Diving the San Juans

by

Dareld & Janine Clark

Evergreen Pacific
Publishing

Seattle, Washington

Printed in Hong Kong

ISBN 0-945265-18-2

Cover photo by Marc Jacobson
Illustrations, graphics, and cover design by Theodore Siebert
Camera work by Precision Screen Graphics

TABLE OF CONTENTS

Acknowledgements 1
About the Authors 2
Preface 3
Introduction 4
A Word About Conservation 5
How To Use This Book 6
Zone Location Chart 9

Zone 1
  1. Allan Island 10
  2. Burrows Island 12
  3. Deception Island 14
  4. Deception Pass 16
  5. Dennis Shoals 18
  6. Fidalgo Head 20
  7. Lawson Reef 22
  8. Sares Head 24
  9. West Point 26
 10. Williamson Rocks 28

Zone 2
 11. Belle Rocks 30
 12. Birds Rocks 32
 13. Colville Island 34
 14. Davidson Rock 36
 15. Goose Island 38
 16. Iceberg Point 40
 17. James Island 42
 18. Kellet Ledge 44
 19. Lawson Rock 46
 20. Long Island 48
 21. Lopez Pass 50
 22. Whale Rocks 52

Zone 3
 23. Battleship Island 54
 24. Bellevue Point 56
 25. Center Reef 58
 26. Charles Point 60
 27. Eagle Point, San Juan Island 62
 28. Johns Island 64
 29. Kellett Bluff 66
 30. Lime Kiln 68
 31. Low Island 70

Zone 3 (cont.)

32. McCracken Point 72
33. Pile Point 74
34. Spieden Bluff 76
35. Turn Point 78

Zone 4

36. Alden Point 80
37. Boundary Pass Marker Buoy 82
38. Eagle Point, Matia Island 84
39. Ewing Island 86
40. Flattop Island 88
41. Johnson Point 90
42. Jones Island 92
43. Lawson Bluff 94
44. Parker Reef 96
45. Point Disney 98
46. Point Doughty 100
47. Puffin Island 102
48. Raccoon Point 104
49. Skipjack Island 106
50. Toe Point 108
51. White Rock 110

Zone 5

52. Carter Point 112
53. Cone Island 114
54. Cypress Reef 116
55. Eagle Cliff 118
56. Eliza Rock 120
57. Hat/Saddlebag Islands 122
58. Lawrence Point 124
59. Peavine Pass 126
60. Strawberry Island 128
61. Towhead Island 130
62. Viti Rocks 132

Index by Dive Sites 135

ACKNOWLEDGEMENTS

Those people that I wish to thank are:

Mike Anderson of Anacortes Diving & Supply. All dives listed in this book were dived by Dareld Clark and/or Mike Anderson. Mike continues to impress me by the breadth and depth of his diving knowledge. He is truly a diver's diver. You can stop at Anacortes Diving & Supply for the latest information on visibility and weather conditions in the Strait. Mike can be reached at (206) 293-2070.

Carl Baird for acting as safety diver for the past two years. I appreciated the fact that Carl was ready and willing to rise early on any weekend morning and travel several long hours just to reach our destination for that sacred slack tide. Carl is a true friend and an excellent diver. Carl is a past officer of the Marker Buoy Dive Club in Seattle.

Harry Truitt of Lighthouse Diving for always taking the time out of his busy schedule to offer words of wisdom and encouragement. His knowledge of the diving industry and his personal diving experience are equaled by few. Harry was also working on the salvage operation of the GOVERNOR. Harry can be reached at (206) 771-2679 in Lynnwood.

Ted Siebert for illustrating and laying out this book from cover to cover. He is a talented artist and has become a very close friend. Ted will be involved in illustrating future publications of the Evergreen Pacific Dive series. He can be reached at (206) 353-3938 in Everett.

ABOUT THE AUTHORS

Dareld Clark is a math/science teacher in the Marysville School District. Dareld has written two diving articles which were published in DIVER Magazine. "Diving the Diamond Knot" was published in August 1986 and "Diving Deception Pass" was published in September of 1987. Dareld holds a PADI DIVEMASTER certification.

Janine Clark is a language arts and social studies teacher in the Marysville School District. Janine and Dareld have also written the book PUGET SOUND SHORE DIVES published in 1988 by Evergreen Pacific Publishing in Seattle.

PREFACE

This book is designed to assist you in locating and planning a rewarding boat dive in the San Juan Islands. Why a boat dive? If you are like most divers in Puget Sound, you have spent countless hours exploring the shore dive sites in your area. You have also discovered the simple fact that diver access to interesting dives from the shore is limited. Once you have made the shore dives that appeal to you, the next logical step is boat diving.

We have tried to provide you with a blend of all the information you will need to successfully plan and complete the boat dive or dives of your choice. Using this guide to plan your dives will help you to become a more aware and experienced diver. This book does not attempt to be a marine biology text or species identification handbook. There are several fine publications of that nature already available. We simply want to offer you an affordable guide to the best boat diving in the San Juan Islands.

We have made every effort to produce an error-free publication. We hope the readers of this book will feel free to send us additional information so that it may be improved. Please address your letters to:

Dareld Clark
c/o Evergreen Pacific Publishing
18002 15th Ave. NE, Suite B
Seattle, WA 98155

A WORD ABOUT CONSERVATION

The first book I bought and read about diving in the San Juan Islands was 141 DIVES by Betty Pratt-Johnson. It was several years later that I had an opportunity to dive one of her most beautifully described dive sites, Lovers Cove. I was shocked and hurt not to find the dive site as she had described it. Had there been a mistake?

I talked to several local resident divers who have been diving the San Juan Islands and Lovers Cove long before the publication of her book. We came to the conclusion that indeed a mistake had been made. The mistake had been made by each of the hundreds of divers who came to the spot each year to take advantage of the natural resource. A few came to look, admire, and photograph, but the majority came to take all they could on each and every dive. This was no conspiracy, no dive boat operation, no commercial harvesting or exporting of our natural resource. Each innocent diver contributed to the demise of, as Betty Pratt-Johnson described it, "...the most beautiful spot I've ever seen."

I have described over 60 dive spots in the San Juan Islands. It is my hope that each of us will learn to take a little less or to stop taking at all. Collect enough fish for only one meal and leave the rest. Seafood is always best when eaten fresh anyway. Buy yourself a set of Mac's Field Guide. They are plastic coated color illustrations of marine invertebrates and coastal fish of the Pacific Northwest. Practice the skills of observation, identification, and classification of different marine creatures. Invest in an inexpensive water-tight camera and practice your photographic skills just below the surface.

Each of us must do our part in protecting the environment and by developing alternative diving activities. Let's learn from the tragedy of Lovers Cove.

INTRODUCTION

It is the rare diver who has never been disappointed in a dive site because it did not contain the variety of plant or animal life he or she had hoped to see. One of the purposes of this book is to help you select dive sites based on a knowledge of the environment and of the plant forms and the vertebrate and invertebrate populations to be found there. Your understanding of the relationship between organisms and their habitat will increase greatly as you follow this method of dive selection and planning.

There are basically three types of habitat that support plant and animal life in Puget Sound: mud, sand, and rock. Mud occurs in protected bays where the currents and wave action are too gentle to wash away the silt deposited by the rivers and streams. Here the life forms reflect the biological adaptations necessary to survive under these conditions. Worms burrow through the mud. Clams anchor their bodies in the ooze and extend their siphons to feed. Snails and slugs travel successfully over the surface by spreading their weight over a proportionately large surface area. As interesting as these adaptations are, most divers prefer a habitat that offers a richer variety of life forms.

A pure sand environment, or sand mixed with pebbles, is the aquatic equivalent to a desert. However, a mixture of organic debris, mud, sand, and pebbles, close enough to the surface to permit photosynthesis, will allow a wide variety of organisms to thrive. Among the creatures that live here are crab, clams, sunflower stars, sea lettuce, and many more. This is usually a favorite habitat for divers.

Eelgrass is actually an independent environment and can occur either in the sand or mud areas. The eelgrass creates its own ecosystem. Its cycles of growth and decay enrich the sand until it can be classified as a mud environment. Eelgrass beds provide abundant food and support a large population of many types of organisms.

Most divers prefer to explore rocky habitats and artificial reefs. These are most common along the Strait of Juan de Fuca and in the San Juan Islands. Here you will find the greatest variety of plant and animal life forms. Colorful sea anemones and basket stars cling to the rocks. Rock fish and greenling hide in the forests of kelp. There is much to see here.

HOW TO USE THIS BOOK

Each site selected is summarized in the same manner for your ease in putting together a safe, enjoyable, and knowledgeable dive. Data for each dive site is divided into four sections.

1. Habitat and Depth

Divers are naturally interested in what they will see at a given site. Therefore, the first questions to ask are "What is the depth?" and "What is the habitat?" These will determine the life forms you will see on the dive. You will encounter rock, sand, and mud environments, alone, and in combinations with one another.

2. Dive Profile

This is a narrative of the dive from the point of entry. We describe what we saw and our general and specific impressions of the area. Only dive sites that proved interesting and enjoyable have been included. We dove dozens of locations which were excluded for one reason or another.

3. Directions

We list only the launch sites that we have used. Other launch locations may be closer to your particular point of departure. Directions should be read through a couple of times to be sure they make sense to you. We also include geographical reference points and compass directions (true, not magnetic). We estimated the distance to each area as accurately as possible. None of these sites is difficult to find. NOAA charts should be used at all times.

4. Hazards

Boat diving demands much more precision and experience than shore diving. Your confidence and equipment must be in ready condition before you go over the side. Boat diving is also much more exciting and adventure-filled than shore diving. It is what you thought scuba diving would be all about.

All of the areas we dove were in high exchange areas. Until you are quite comfortable with boat diving, all of your dives should be done on the slack. Wait until you gain confidence and experience before you begin to explore drift diving.

Your boat diving activities should begin with a qualified instructor who is familiar with local currents and who has already dived the area. Go with professionals until you are confident and competent. They are always ready and willing to help and guide you at whatever your level of expertise.

All of the dives in this book were "live boat" dives, that is, the boat was not anchored and there was a non-diving boat operator on board at all times. Don't forget that boat traffic is an ever-present possibility in the San Juan Islands.

Abiding by a few common sense rules on all of the listed dives should minimize any safety problems for boats or divers. 1. When navigating, always use the appropriate NOAA chart. Steer clear of the noted rocky areas and reefs. 2. Do not run your boat too close to any of the islands, rocks, or reefs, especially during low tide. 3. Before setting out, check with your favorite dive shop for the latest information on visibility and weather conditions in the area you are planning to dive. 4. Always fly a diver flag to alert the constant boat traffic to your presence. 5. Plan to ascend from your dive with at least 500 psi in case you run into difficulty, or so you can respond appropriately if your buddy needs help.

ZONE LOCATION CHART

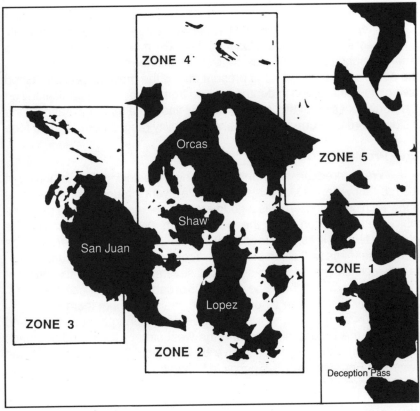

① ALLAN ISLAND

Habitat and Depth

There is loose shale almost all the way around the island, especially on the west side which faces Rosario Strait. The more protected sides have a sandy/muddy bottom. Below that, shale mixed with sand/mud ledges is the dominant habitat. Kelp is present during the growing season. Good diving may be enjoyed in depths ranging from 20 to 100 ft., particularly on the northwest side of the island. You will find more mud and sand on the inside where the currents are weaker. Visibility ranges from 12 to 20 feet.

Dive Profile

We entered the water on the most northwesterly point, just inside of the rock shown on NOAA chart 18421. We swam through the kelp and met a few kelp greenling. This is a good area for shrimp and red sea gherkins which find protection along the rocky bottom. We enjoyed watching the gherkins feed by licking the food off of their tentacles. Many pecten scallops may be seen, as well as an occasional rock scallop. Red sea cucumbers, brown rockfish, great sculpin, sea squirt, several varieties of crab, and giant red sea urchins also inhabit the area. Lots of cabezon and lingcod live here, and you will usually see a number of the seals who hunt them.

You can dive this site with relative ease during both summer and winter. If the wind is blowing and the west side of the island becomes choppy, you should alter your dive by changing to the more protected waters of Burrows Bay. It is possible to drift from one end of the island to the other during a tidal exchange.

Directions

Allan Island is located on the west side of Fidalgo Island, south of Fidalgo Head, and just south of Burrows Island. You can launch your boat at Deception Pass, Flounder Bay, Washington Park, or Cap Sante in Anacortes.

Allan Island was named for a U.S. naval captain who was killed in the War of 1812 with Britain. Small bays around the island are fine places for a lunch stop in good weather. Washington Park is a nice spot to spend the afternoon after your dive. Deception Pass is equally close, accessible by boat, and worth a visit.

Hazards

This is a favorite boating and fishing area. Boats traveling to and from Deception Pass will likely pass on the inside of the islands to avoid the afternoon winds and rougher water on the strait.

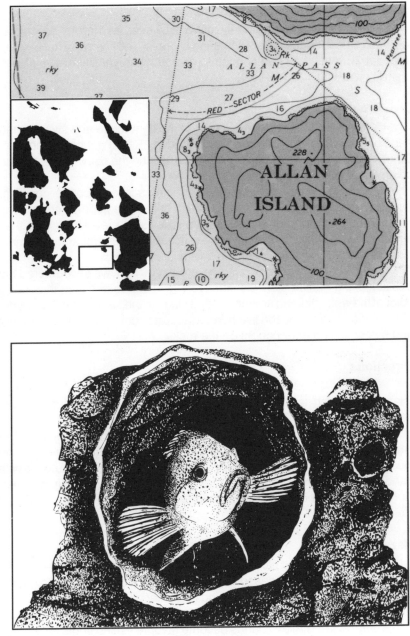

Quillback Rockfish

② BURROWS ISLAND LIGHTHOUSE

Habitat and Depth

The habitat here is primarily rocky. However, as the bluff descends, the less vertical ledges collect a frosting of gravel and fine silt. There is kelp to about 20 feet. You can choose to dive at whatever depth you prefer. Visibility is about 12 to 15 feet.

Dive Profile

We entered the water just south of the lighthouse and swam to the edge of the kelp bed. There we descended to 25 ft. to get below the kelp. Our dive continued in a southerly direction around the point. Note that the southwest side is extremely deep.

As for sea creatures, there were pecten scallops, copper rockfish, and red sea gherkins. The red sea cucumbers were good-sized and tiny crabs used them for hiding places. We saw quite a few shrimp but they flitted so quickly around us that we were not able to determine what variety they were. Several kelp greenling swam close by us.

At the deepest point of our dive, around 80 feet, we encountered the exotic looking basket star. Its soft, ivory skin contrasted with the snowy color of the white plumed anemones that clung to the same rocky formation. Many lingcod and cabezon live here, as well as some octopuses. You will find lots of fishing gear caught on the rocks.

Directions

Burrows Island is between Allan Island and Fidalgo Head on Fidalgo Island. You can launch your boat at Deception Pass, Flounder Bay, Washington Park, or Cap Sante in Anacortes.

After your dive, you would be wise to choose the east side of the island to anchor for lunch as it is protected from winds from the north and west. However, Burrows Bay is open to south winds. There are coves with sandy beaches on Allen Island that make good stops in fair weather. Burrows Island and Bay were named for a U.S. naval hero, Lt. William Burrows.

Hazards

Avoid running too close to Burrows Island. Bull kelp is present on the rocks during the growing season. The western face of the island is exposed to the stronger tidal influence and winds of Rosario Strait. Exercise caution. There are strong currents and riptides just south of the lighthouse point.

Burrows and Allan Islands become favorite fishing spots for anglers when the winds are too brisk in the strait.

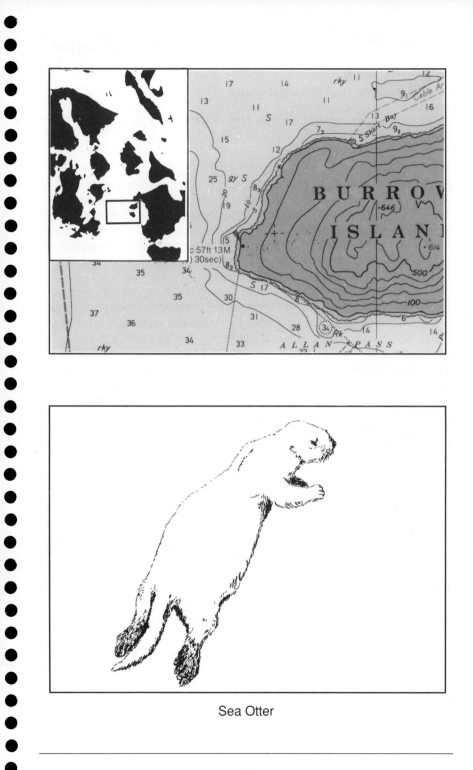

Sea Otter

(3) **DECEPTION ISLAND**

Habitat and Depth

This is an area of rocks and ledges. There is a natural rocky reef that reaches from Rosario Beach on Fidalgo Island to Deception Island. You can choose your most comfortable depth for diving. The visibility is 12 to 15 feet. Kelp is present.

Dive Profile

We dove on the tail end of a flood tide, jumping from the boat on the west side of the island. The bull kelp there is thick so we dove down just before we reached it and settled on the bottom at about 40 feet. It was easy to circle the island. We heard boats passing on the north side on their way to the San Juans, so we increased our depth to 60 feet. After we were down for 25 minutes, the current began to ebb. We surfaced on the west side of the island when the current became stronger.

Diving a rocky habitat in a high current area is always exciting and rewarding. Against a beautiful background display of white plumed and pink-tipped anemones, we noticed a good-sized lingcod. Later, we saw a couple of smaller ones and some cabezon. We scanned the barnacle-encrusted rocks for a crevice that might hide an octopus. At first all we found were orange cup coral, sun stars, the largest about eight inches, and some big purple stars. We sighted the ever present pecten scallops and a couple of basket stars. Finally, our search was rewarded. An octopus was wedged in a concealing cave. It stayed put, but we estimated its size to be about ten feet from tip to tip.

Directions

Deception Island is the western-most island in Deception Pass State Park. It takes its name from the pass. It is approximately one mile west of the spectacular bridge that links Fidalgo and Whidbey Islands. The most convenient launching sites are Cornet Bay and Bowman Bay. At the latter, you may experience difficulty reloading a larger boat at low tide. Either bay is a good spot to relax and have lunch after your dive.

Hazards

Avoid drifting your boat too close to the island. Be especially careful of your boat near the west point of the island where the reef extends out. There are shoals to the north.

High currents and strong winds are always a great concern in the Deception Pass area. Fishing and boating traffic will be at their heaviest whenever conditions are perfect for diving.

Plan a stop at Deception Pass State Park after your dive. (See Deception Pass dive.)

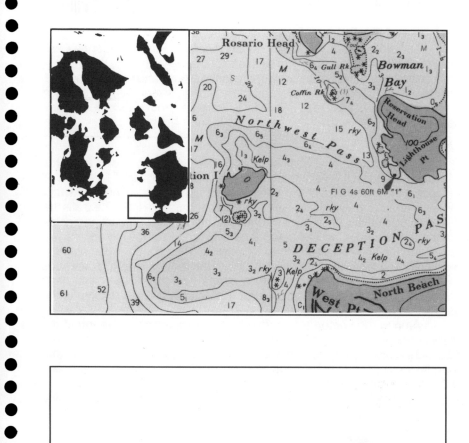

Orca Whale

④ DECEPTION PASS

Habitat and Depth

The sides of the main channels of Deception Pass and Canoe Pass are rocky and fairly vertical. The west end of Canoe Island and the western end of the pass (beyond the bridge) are less vertical, and you will find rock mixed with silt. The depth is beyond that of sports divers. We have limited our depths to 60 to 80 feet. Visibility is limited to from 5 to 15 feet. Kelp is present.

Dive Profile

Our preferred dive begins about 50 feet west of the bridge on the Whidbey Island side. We entered the water just before slack. This allowed us to feel the movement of the water at the precise moment of slack water as we made our way to the bridge. This area teems with life. The walls are like a living mosaic. The background is formed by the encrusting pecten sponges and barnacles. Color and texture are added by the tiny orange cup coral and the aptly named staghorn bryozoa. Pink-tipped, white plumed, and orange anemones thrive here. One of the most interesting creatures we encountered was the tiny ostrich plume hydroid. It seems to have graceful, brownish-black feathers, but it is actually a close relative of the jellyfish.

Among the pecten and purple hinged rock scallops, we found the eery protrusions of dead man's fingers. Some of these warty sponges were ten inches high. Hairy sea squirts and giant red sea urchins (some were purple) were abundant. We noted brown rockfish, quillback rockfish, and a number of kelp greenling as we drifted.

As the flood began, we were pushed faster and faster through the pass. We moved under the bridge and east along the semi-vertical wall. We made a controlled ascent to the surface along the wall, listening for the sounds of boat traffic. Once on the surface, we relaxed and waited to be picked up by our dive boat. It was an exhilarating dive.

Directions

Deception Pass is a two mile long passage between Whidbey and Fidalgo Islands. You can launch your boat at Cornet Bay, Bowman Bay, or the other launch sites previously mentioned. (See loading information, Deception Island dive.)

Deception Pass was named by British explorer George Vancouver who at first thought it was a bay rather than a pass. It would be worthwhile to read about the Deception Pass area before making a trip there. Plan on visiting the park itself. There are over 250 campsites, with restrooms, boat moorage and launching.

Hazards

Extreme currents, turbulence, up-wellings, down-drafts, kelp, and heavy boat traffic make this a potentially hazardous dive spot. This is a terrific dive, but we strongly recommend that you only attempt it on a guided dive tour or with divers experienced in diving the pass.

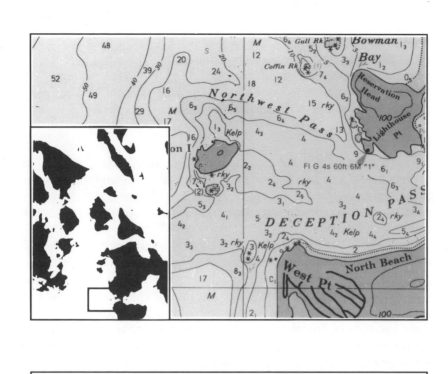

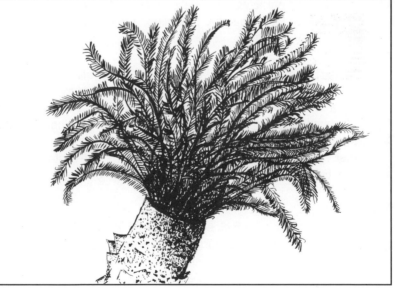

Banded Feather Duster

⑤ DENNIS SHOALS

Habitat and Depth

This is an area of rocky ledges and bluffs. There is a reef, marked by a buoy on its west side, which is only three feet below the surface on minus tides. You will find kelp during the growing season. You can select your preferred depth. Visibility is 12 to 15 feet.

Dive Profile

To avoid running too close to the rocks, we entered the water just north of the kelp bed on the end of an ebbing tide. The current carried us to the buoy. We followed the anchor line down to the bottom where we readjusted our equipment and regrouped. We then proceeded toward the south side of the shoal.

Diving in the middle of Rosario Strait is always exciting. The rock walls were solid with sea anemones of all colors and sizes, even some green ones which get their color from the algae which live in their tissues. There were purple sea urchins, which are smaller and shorter spined than the purple variety of the giant red sea urchin. In addition to some creeping pedal cucumbers, tiny, but colorful with bright red tentacles, we also saw many red sea gherkins. As is usual throughout this area, there were pecten and rock scallops. We also saw basket stars and the tiny black and white brittle star. On this particular dive we were lucky enough to see a variety of fish: lingcod, cabezon, painted greenling, and black cod.

Directions

Dennis Shoals is located SSW of Allan Island. It is 220 degrees from the closest point on Allan Island and about 500 yards off the south shore. It is 0.6 of a mile to the northwest (327 degrees) from Williamson Rocks. You can launch at Deception Pass, Flounder Bay, Washington Park, or Cap Sante in Anacortes.

After your dive, you may want to relax in the more protected waters of Burrows Bay or visit Washington Park or Deception Pass Park.

Hazards

Keep from running too close to the shoal, especially on a high tide when it may be hidden. Wind, currents, open water, and extreme depths can all present hazards. An enormous amount of water passes through this area. Always dive on the best slack of the day. Be alert for fishing nets.

Kelp can be present, and there is a large volume of boat traffic.

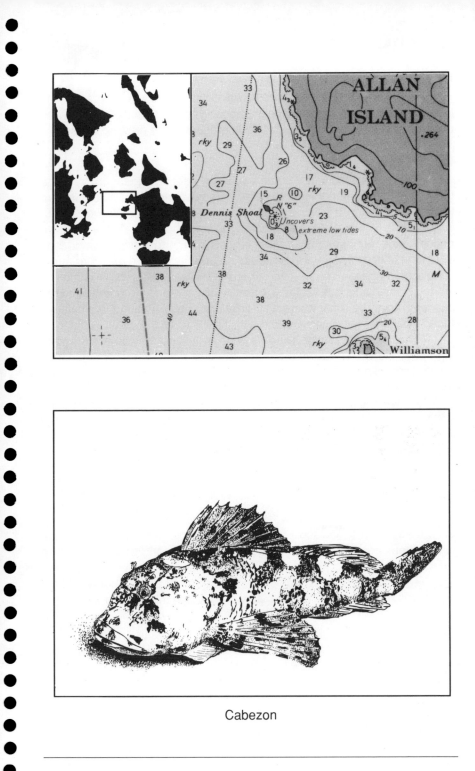

Cabezon

Habitat and Depth

This is primarily a rocky wall; however, sand and silt collect along the ledges and outcroppings. You can choose your most comfortable diving depth. Visibility is 5 to 15 feet. Kelp is present in the growing season.

Dive Profile

We entered the water on an ebb slack right next to the rocky ledge that is just to the west of Flounder Bay. We descended and swam toward the wall and explored the creatures of the lower tidal zone. We worked our way down to 60 feet as we heard boats passing above us. As we went, we noticed pink nudibranchs on the ledges near the white plumed sea anemones. We saw several sea stars: a brightly colored rose star and a couple of vermillion stars. There were a few sea cucumbers along the ledges, pecten and rock scallops, a colony of giant red sea urchins, and red cancer crab. The most interesting creatures were a pair of wolfeels we found living in a rocky crevice.

The tide began to flood and we gently made our way toward the point of Fidalgo Head. There were a number of fish in the area. We identified painted greenling, cabezon, and a lingcod as they swam by. Hiding among the kelp, we saw graceful kelp crab and northern kelp crab.

As we rounded the point, the depth began to decrease and the habitat changed from the rock wall to a muddy bottom. As you would expect, the animal life changed to compensate. Here we found sea cucumbers and many sunflower stars in brilliant shades of pink, orange and purple. The crab were the red rock variety.

Directions

Fidalgo Head, the most westerly point of Fidalgo Island, was named for a member of Francisco Eliza's Spanish exploration party. You can launch your boat at Flounder Bay, Washington Park, or Cap Sante in Anacortes.

Take time to visit Washington Park before or after your dive. It's a nice place to relax and enjoy the view or to watch the rabbit population.

Hazards

We dove 100 yards southwest of the western tip. Because diving this area on a falling tide will draw you into Rosario Strait, the best time to dive is on the slack or on a slight flood.

There is a lot of boat traffic from nearby Skyline Marina. Stay close to the wall and well away from the boating/fishing lanes. Underwater visibility can be poor.

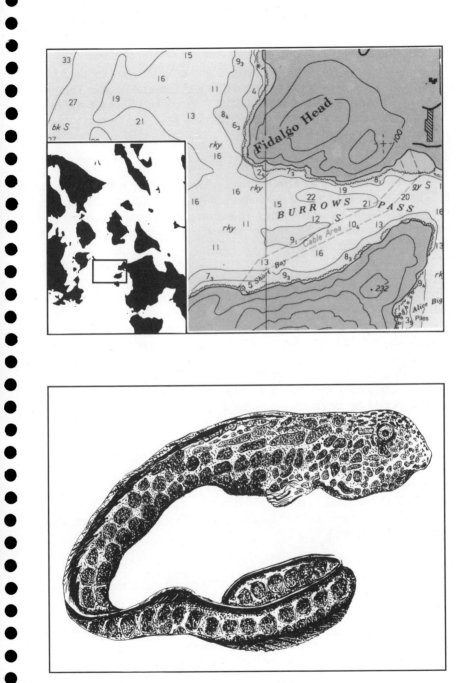

Wolfeel (juvenile)

⑦ LAWSON REEF

Habitat and Depth

This is a rocky reef with ledges and drop-offs and marked by a lighted bell buoy. Do not confuse this dive with Lawson Rock in Thatcher Pass or Lawson Bluff on Sucia Island. You can choose your most comfortable maximum depth. Visibility varies from 5 to 15 feet. Kelp is present during the growing season.

Dive Profile

We chose to dive Lawson Reef on an ebb slack with a moderate tidal exchange. We entered the water just south of the light and explored the rocky area on the south side. This area gets deep very quickly. We worked our way down to 50 - 60 feet as we made our way around the steep drop-off that surrounds the reef.

Brilliant blue-striped sea perch schooled among the cliffs, reminding us of tropical waters. Kelp greenling glided by at a more leisurely pace. We glimpsed a large lingcod before it disappeared from the rock where it had been perched.

The rocks themselves supported many smaller creatures. Glassy sea squirts mingled with the giant barnacles and the pecten and rock scallops. Wearing bits of seaweed and sponge, a decorator crab made its way among the cup coral and rosy encrusting bryozoa. Basket stars glowed whitely next to purple sea urchins, red sea gherkins, and orange sea anemones as they all clung to the rocky walls.

Directions

Lawson Reef is approximately 269 degrees from West Point at Deception Pass State Park, or roughly 2.9 miles from the bridge at Deception Pass. You can launch your boat at Cornet Bay or Bowman Bay. (See loading information, Deception Island dive.)

Plan a stop at Deception Pass State Park after your dive. (See Deception Pass dive.)

Hazards

Avoid running too close to the bell buoy. If you have launched at Cornet Bay, do not approach too close to West Point.

This dive is almost in the center of Rosario Strait. You need to dive Lawson Reef with an experienced buddy. Wind, high current, and occasional poor visibility are common hazards.

Kelp can be present, and heavy boat traffic is a constant hazard. In addition, there are often fishing nets, so be alert and be sure to carry a knife.

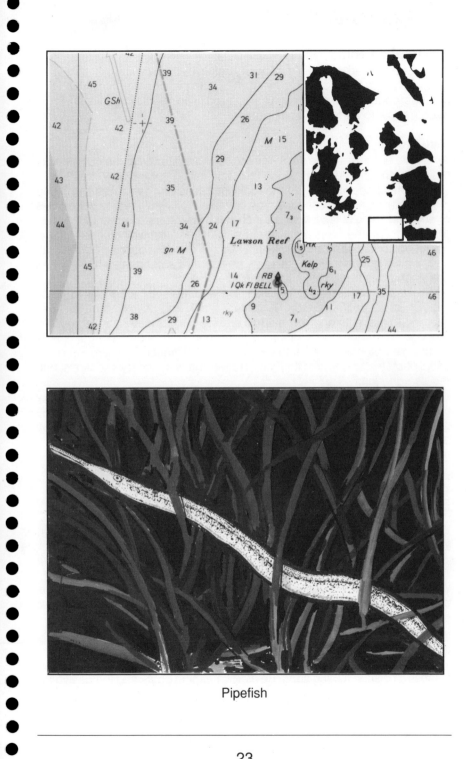

Pipefish

⑧ SARES HEAD

Habitat and Depth

Sares Head is a steep rock wall, broken by many small gravel ledges. There is a light to moderate current. You can pick the depth at which you are most comfortable diving and be assured of an interesting dive. Visibility averages 12 to 15 feet. Kelp is present.

Dive Profile

We began the dive on an ebbing tide. We started at the north end of the head and drifted south along the rock wall at depths of 40 to 60 feet.

Lots of sea life cling to the rocky surfaces and swim nearby. If you look carefully under the ledges, you can see the tiny skeletons of colonies of sea firs, usually less than an inch tall. Sea stars are plentiful. Most abundant are the ivory basket stars, gray and brown varieties of the ubiquitous brittle star and purple sea stars. We saw a banded hermit crab carrying his home, a whelk shell, as he scurried among the white plumed sea anemones and violet encrusting sponge.

As we drifted along the wall, we encountered a school of black rockfish of respectable size. A solitary black and yellow china rockfish seemed to make its home in a small crevice surrounded by giant red sea urchins. We kept a safe distance from the stinging tentacles of a pale orange sea blubber. We also saw some small lingcod. There were the usual pecten scallops with their pink edged shells, a few rock scallops, and red sea gherkins.

More then one pair of wolfeels make their homes in the rocky crevices. Their fierce faces cover up a shy nature. We knew that this was good habitat for octopuses so we searched carefully. Our hunt was rewarded when we found an octopus holed up in what appeared to be a mini-cave.

Directions

This projecting headland, located between Deception Pass and Fidalgo Head, runs just south of Biz Point and north of Northwest Island. You can choose to launch your boat at Deception Pass, Flounder Bay, Washington Park, or Cap Sante in Anacortes.

You can stop at Burrows Bay which is protected from winds from the west and north but is exposed to winds from the south, or plan a visit to Washington Park or Deception Pass State Park. Sares Head sounds exotic, but it was actually named for a member of the Charles Wilkes exploratory expedition.

Hazards

Kelp is present during the growing season. From Biz Point to Sares Head is a popular fishing spot. Be alert for fishing boats and the possibility of gill nets.

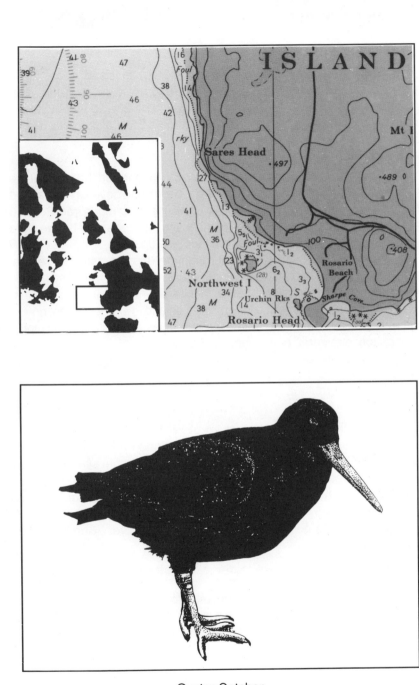

Oyster Catcher

Habitat and Depth

A rocky reef runs from West Point to Deception Island. Close to the point the habitat is sand/gravel. Bull kelp is present most of the year. Visibility is 5 to 15 feet. Maximum depth would be 20 - 30 feet out to the rocks which bare on a low tide. It is 17 fathoms SSW of the point itself.

Dive Profile

We chose to dive on the end of a flood. We entered the water at the northwest side of the point, swam toward the reef, and dove as we reached the kelp. Working our way from SSE to NNW, we descended from 20 to 60 feet and explored both sides of the reef. As the tide began to ebb, we were pushed around West Point to our boat for pick-up.

As we worked our way down through the kelp, we disturbed several small kelp crab. There is a lot of life sheltered by the reef itself. The anemones were especially colorful: white plumed, orange, and pink-tipped. Sea urchins came in a variety of sizes and in shades of red, green, and purple. Rocks were covered with barnacles, ribbed keyhole limpits, giant chiton, cup coral, and staghorn bryozoa.

The reef harbors several kinds of rockfish including copper, brown, and quillback.

Directions

West Point is the northwest tip of Whidbey Island at the end of Deception Pass. It is part of Deception Pass State Park. You can launch your boat at Cornet Bay, Bowman Bay, or any of the other sites previously mentioned. (See loading information, Deception Island dive.) West Point can also be reached by an inflatable craft launched from Deception Pass State Park.

The park is a good place to relax after your dive. (See Deception Pass dive.)

Hazards

Keep from running too close to West Point itself. The current is quite strong and visibility can be poor. This is an area of very heavy boat traffic. Stay close to the reef and use your compass. Exit only at West Point or Deception Island.

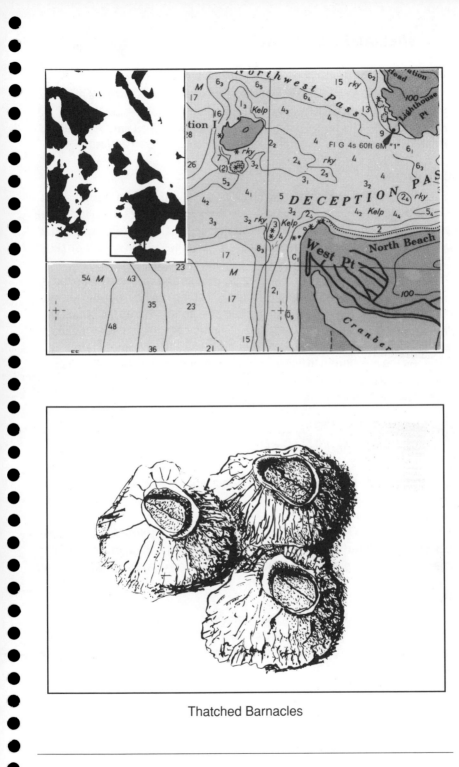

Thatched Barnacles

⑩ WILLIAMSON ROCKS

Habitat and Depth

As the name implies, Williamson Rocks are a rocky habitat made up of ledges and cliffs. The rocks are marked on the south side by a lighted gong buoy. Kelp is present in the growing season. You can choose your own most comfortable maximum depth. Visibility is 5 to 20 feet.

Dive Profile

We were diving on an ebb slack and entered the water on the east side of the rocks where you will see a little cove. We descended to 15 feet and worked our way around and through the rocks. The kelp surrounded us and it was necessary to swim amidst it. It sheltered some northern kelp crab.

We spent a lot of time examining the nooks and crannies of the rocks. They were covered with many of the typical life forms—barnacles, cup coral, encrusting bryozoa. White plumed anemones shared the space with little creeping pedal cucumbers and colonies of giant red sea urchins in several colors. Graceful basket stars also make their homes here.

As the tide began to flood, we were pushed north toward Allan Island and our boat. We sighted more fish than usual on this dive. There were lingcod, cabezon, black cod, and kelp greenling.

Directions

Williamson Rocks are 0.5 miles (200 degrees) south of Allan Island and 1.5 miles (289 degrees) from Biz Point. The rocks are bare and marked on the south side by a buoy. You can launch your boat at Washington Park, Flounder Bay, Bowman Bay, or Cornet Bay. (See loading information, Deception Island dive.)

Williamson Rocks were named for a member of the Wilkes expedition which explored the area. After your dive, the small bays around Allan Island make good places to anchor in fair weather, relax, and have a meal.

Hazards

Williamson Rocks are in the open water of Rosario Strait. Wind and strong currents are always hazards. Dive this area on a slack tide only. Be alert for shifts in current velocity and direction. The water surrounding the rocks is extremely deep.

This area receives a lot of boat traffic. There can be old fishing nets around so watch out for them and carry a knife.

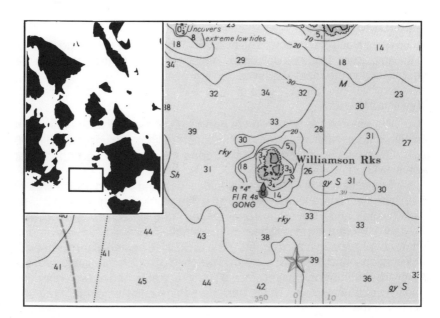

White Frilled Anemone

(11) BELLE ROCK

Habitat and Depth

Belle Rock is characterized by a very high current exchange on all of its craggy sides. Depth is unlimited. Visibility is from 15 to 25 feet. To the west, which is the most shallow side, is gravel.

Dive Profile

We entered the water on the north side of the rock at the end of an ebb flood tide. After we swam to the concrete light, we descended to 50 feet. Gradually we made our way around the rock and ascended near where we had entered.

The east side of Belle Rock is fairly steep and offered a wide variety of animal life. There were many large white plumed anemones, perhaps 14 inches tall, and a few orange ones, or sea pumpkins, clinging to the rock. We saw a banded hermit crab wearing a whelk shell make his way among algae-covered dead man's fingers. The rocks also hosted giant barnacles, rock scallops, and dusty rose-colored patches of rock encrusting bryozoa. Several beautiful ivory basket stars, a spiny rose star, and red sea gherkins made a colorful display. There were very large colonies of giant red sea urchins in the crevices.

Moving about in their own peculiar fashion were pecten scallops with pecten sponges attached to their upper valves. Black rockfish schooled nearby, and we glimpsed brown rockfish and lingcod. There were a number of cabezon and kelp greenling. We encountered a few water jellyfish about 4 inches in diameter.

On the east side, which drops off in ledges, there is a large chain, probably from an anchor, at about 20 feet. We followed it to 95 feet where it dropped over another ledge and kept heading for Never Never Land.

Directions

Belle Rock is located 2 miles west of Fidalgo Head (270 degrees) and 0.5of a mile northeast of Bird Rocks (38 degrees). You can launch your boat at Deception Pass, Flounder Bay, Washington Park, or Cap Sante in Anacortes.

On your first few trips to the Islands, you should plan on visiting Deception Pass State Park, Washington Park, James Island State Park, and Spencer Spit State Park, all of which have moorage and good facilities.

Hazards

Belle Rock is bare at extreme low tide and is marked by a light. Avoid running too close to the rock. Because of its position in roughly the middle of Rosario Strait, Belle Rock can be exposed to extreme tidal action and winds. It is very deep on three sides. If the wind kicks up in the afternoon, it is only a short run to protection behind James Island.

Minke Whale

Habitat and Depth

Do not confuse this dive with Bird Rock in San Juan Channel. This is primarily a rocky habitat with some loose shale. You can choose your most comfortable maximum depth. Visibility averages about 15 feet. There is kelp during the growing season.

Dive Profile

We entered the water on an ebb slack on the south side of the rocks which are marked on NOAA chart 18421. We descended to 15 feet and followed our plan which was to circle the rocks. Our depths varied to suit the terrain, but for the most part, we never dropped much below 60 feet.

Right away we noticed the dark orange tentacles of many red sea gherkins protruding from small crevices. They were a colorful contrast to the solid walls of white plumed sea anemones and a variety of sea urchins. Looking more closely, we found the tiny creeping pedal cucumbers, bright red, but only about 2 inches long. Orange cup coral and staghorn bryozoa also covered part of the surface.

Large numbers of the small gregarious jellyfish seemed to float out of nowhere. Pecten scallops were all around, as well as a few rock scallops. One of the most interesting creatures was a 6 or 7 inch galathoid crab that looked like a tiny lobster. At one point we came upon black bass and yellow tail as well as an octopus. We also saw cabezon, a large lingcod, and many seals.

This area has lots of old practice bombs left from the 1960's and 70's when Whidbey Island Naval Air Station flew training missions here. The bombs are not live.

Directions

Bird Rocks are just 0.5 mile SW of Belle Rock (218 degrees) and 2.4 miles WSW of Fidalgo Head (259 degrees). You can launch your boat at Deception Pass, Flounder Bay, Washington Park, or Cap Sante in Anacortes.

As its name implies, Bird Rocks are part of the bird refuge administered by the U.S. Fish and Wildlife Service. Keep your boat well clear so the seabirds are not disturbed.

(See Belle Rock dive for facilities information.)

Hazards

Charts clearly mark the rocky areas and depths. Avoid running too close to the rocks themselves. Bird Rocks are located in the middle of Rosario Strait and are, therefore, subject to extreme tidal exchanges and high current conditions as well as occasional unpredictable winds. Lopez Pass is a close retreat from heavy afternoon winds.

Mosshead Warbonnet

COLVILLE ISLAND

Habitat and Depth

Colville Island is a small, rocky habitat off the southeast shore of Lopez Island. There is some shale, and there are rocky ledges on the deeper south side. Bull kelp is present in season. You can choose your most comfortable maximum depth. Visibility ranges from 15 to 25 feet.

Dive Profile

We entered the water on a high ebb just west of the kelp bed located on NOAA chart 18421. Our first descent was to 30 feet. After exploring at that level for awhile, we dropped to 40 feet, and finally to 60. During the whole dive, we drifted to the east on the falling tide. We exited just east of the island.

On our initial descent we passed through some kelp. We glimpsed greenling and several graceful kelp crab. At the shallow end of our dive, we saw copper rockfish. A bit deeper was a china rockfish which seemed to claim a small hole under a ledge for its territory.

The walls of the island were covered with white plumed anemone, lots of sea urchins, red sea gherkins, and cup coral. There were a few rock scallops and many pecten scallops. We spotted a hermit crab with an odd-looking shell. Closer examination revealed that an orange-brown hermit sponge had encrusted and gradually replaced the original shell. You will find abalone and octopuses here as well.

The largest creatures we encountered were a couple of shy, although fierce-appearing, wolfeels. They were reluctant to leave their lair, but appeared to be about 6 feet in length.

Directions

Colville Island is located 5.9 miles west (274 degrees) of Deception Island and 0.47 of a mile SW (225 degrees) of Pt. Colville on Lopez Island. You can launch your boat at Deception Pass, Flounder Bay, Washington Park, or Cap Sante in Anacortes.

Colville Island, named for a governor of the Hudson's Bay Company, is the largest bird refuge administered by the U.S. Fish and Wildlife Service in the area. Many species of seabirds nest or stop here. Stay well clear of the Island in order not to disturb the birds.

The far southern reaches of Lopez Island are very rugged and there are no good rest stops in the immediate vicinity of Colville Island. Griffin Bay Recreation Site is a fairly short run across the San Juan Channel. It has limited moorage, camping, picnicking, restrooms, and water. Or, you might choose to head for James Island. (See James Island dive for facilities information.)

Hazards

Be extremely cautious around the many rocky areas on the southern end of Lopez Island. This is both a fishing area and a high traffic area for boaters heading for the San Juan Channel.

Winds can make Rosario Strait quite rough in the afternoon. Mackaye Harbor offers protected anchorage in 25 to 30 feet of water. Barlow Bay can shelter small craft but is rather tricky at low tide due to rocks.

8₄ (4 ★

100

Pt Colville

1₅

9₁ 4₁

6₄

7₄ 4₂

9₄

★ 6

rky

9₁

7★

5

7₄

Kelp 9₁

6

3₅

9₁ rky

S

7₄

8₃

7₃

13

9 Castle I 12

9

11

12

12

5

12

14

15

18

26

11

11

23

27

9₄

9₃ Colville I 16

13

2

3₁

5₂

6₂

23

23

26

16

6₃ 2₁ 5 7₃

13

Fl 4sec 15ft

34

15

23

15

rky 7₃ 14

9₄ Davidson Rk

34

36

18

26

35

38

36

32

27

42

36

37

37

38

33

32

29

32

48

46

42

37

31

37

Arctic Tern

35

Habitat and Depth

This is an area of many rocky ledges. Davidson Rock is marked by a light. Depth is unlimited so you can choose your most comfortable maximum. Visibility is about 15 to 40 feet. The kelp is heavy.

Dive Profile

We dove on a low ebb and entered the water just south of the light marker located on NOAA chart 18421. The rock formations are outstanding and make this a worthwhile sightseeing dive. The kelp bed is quite large and kelp greenling are abundant there.

Davidson Rock is covered by a great variety of sea life. In addition to the walls of white plumed anemones, we saw several large green anemones. They live by themselves in crevices and were about 8 inches in diameter. Under the many ledges we found colonies of tiny sea firs. Giant barnacles and rose-colored rock encrusting bryozoa covered part of the rocks. In places we found yellowish dead man's fingers about 10 inches tall and reddish brown gum boot Chiton about 8 inches long.

Giant red sea urchins pack the crevices while the green urchins appeared more on the surface of the rocks. Puget Sound king crab live here. We examined a hairy sea squirt and found that its brownish color comes from the silt that clings to its yellow body. There were both pecten and rock scallops and abalone. We saw some cabezon and lingcod and black bass by the schools.

The highlight of the dive was finding an octopus out of its lair. This specimen was about 6 feet. We also found lots of lost fishing tackle and some old batteries from the light.

Directions

Davidson Rock is located 0.34 of a mile east of Colville Island (l08 degrees) and 5.65 miles from Deception Island (273 degrees). You can launch your boat at Deception Pass, Flounder Bay, Washington Park, or Cap Sante in Anacortes.

Davidson Rock was named for Capt. George Davidson who charted much of Puget Sound. There are no good rest stops in the immediate vicinity of this rugged area. (See Colville Island dive for facilities information.)

Hazards

Davidson Rock bares at low tide. Do not run too close to it. Be on the alert for fishing nets.

If the wind comes up, see Colville Island dive for shelter information.

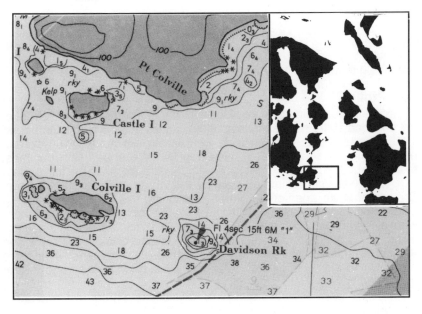

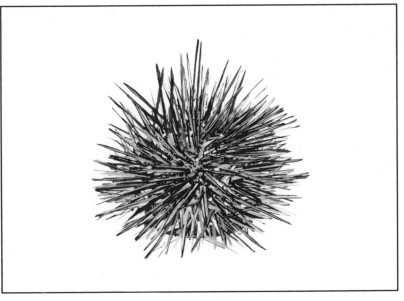

Purple Sea Urchin

⑮　GOOSE ISLAND

Habitat and Depth

Goose Island is located on the east side of San Juan Island about 0.5 mile north of Cattle Point. It is an area of rocky ledges with many caves and crevices. You can choose your most comfortable maximum depth. Visibility is 20 to 45 feet. There is a kelp bed.

Dive Profile

We dove on an absolute slack tide and entered the water in front of the kelp bed at the northeast point of the island, as shown on NOAA chart 18421. The currents here can be dangerous. We descended to 60 feet and explored the same area at varying depths. We ended with our most shallow, about 20 feet, in order to be near the surface when the tide turned.

We were struck immediately by the vibrant color of the life here. Crowds of white anemones, green anemones, sea pumpkins, and cup coral hugged the rocks. Deadman's fingers protruded oddly, and there were clusters of vari-colored plume worms in the rock fissures. We saw lots of pecten scallops and some rock scallops and abalone. Purple sea urchins, an ivory toned basket star, and red sea gherkins added even more color. Given the usually good visibility, this is a great spot for underwater photography.

There were several varieties of rockfish, kelp greenling, and some lingcod as well. Lost fishing gear is a common find.

Directions

Goose Island is located 1.39 miles (312 degrees) from Long Island and 3.47 miles (164 degrees) from Pear Pt. You can launch your boat at Deception Pass, Flounder Bay, Washington Park, or Cap Sante in Anacortes. If you are ferrying your boat to the Islands, you can launch at Roche Harbor Boatel, Snug Harbor Marina, or San Juan County Park, all on San Juan Island; or Rosario, Deer Harbor, Terrill Beach, or West Beach on Orcas Island.

The many bays and coves of southeast San Juan Island are good places to anchor for lunch.

Goose Island is a biological preserve owned by the Nature Conservancy. Its vegetation is much the same as it was in pioneer days. It somehow escaped being overgrazed by settlers' sheep.

Hazards

Avoid the kelp and rocks which are exposed on a low tide on the west side of the island. The major concerns are the swift currents. Normal ebb and flood run at about 2.6 knots, but a maximum flood can run at 5 knots. This area can produce rips and eddies similar to the ones in Deception Pass.

Wind and fishing boats, especially salmon sport fishers, make this a heads-up place to dive. You will find lots of downriggers and other gear on the steep drop-off. Winds can make Haro Strait quite rough in the afternoon. (See Colville Island dive for shelter information.)

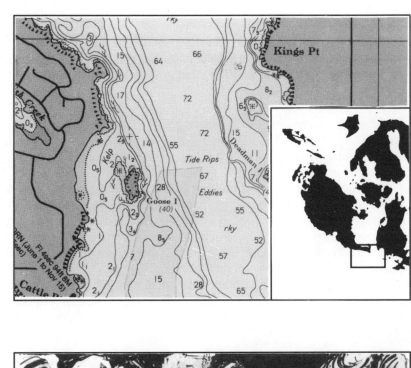

California Mussels

Habitat Depth

Iceberg Point is marked by a navigational beacon. You will find gravel, rock, and loose shale in this combined habitat. Depth is maximum on the outer point. Visibility is 15 to 20 feet. Kelp is always present.

Dive Profile

We entered the water on a high ebb just off the light that is marked on NOAA chart 18421. The kelp was loaded with life. We found northern kelp crab, kelp greenling, perch, a decorator crab decked out in kelp, daisy brittle star, and shrimp.

We descended to 40 feet, took our time exploring, caught the running tide, and exited east of Iceberg Point. There was lots to see here. The rocks supported the usual colorful marine life: large white plumed anemones, purple and green sea urchins, abalone, pecten scallops, and red sea cucumbers. We found a reddish gum boot or giant chiton, probably about 8 inches long and the rather insignificant looking glassy sea squirt. This area is home to the area's largest and fastest species of sea star, the sunflower star. These are active predators. The largest we saw was about 2 1/2 feet across. Among the rocks we observed bass, quillback rockfish, and a school of black rockfish.

Directions

Iceberg Point is located 3.26 miles from Davidson Rock (278 degrees) and 1.47 miles from Long Island (137 degrees). You can launch your boat at Deception pass, Flounder Bay, Washington Park, or Cap Sante in Anacortes.

The land surrounding Iceberg Point is a light house reserve and has a navigational beacon. Rugged cliffs surround an expanse of tidal flat on the south side of Iceberg Point. There is good anchorage on the east side of nearby Iceberg Island which is an undeveloped state park. Both Iceberg Point and Iceberg Island were named for the evidence of glacial action carved into their surfaces.

Hazards

There are rocks around Iceberg Point. Rocky areas are marked and should be carefully noted. Be alert for fishing nets.

Winds can sometimes be a problem and the swell can make a dive inadvisable. (See Colville Island dive for shelter information.)

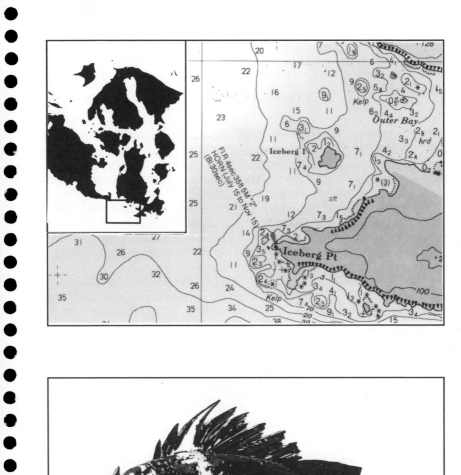

China Rockfish

Habitat and Depth

Here is a rocky habitat with sheer walls, many ledges, and some shale. You can choose your maximum depth, depending upon your experience. Visibility is from 10 to 20 feet.

Dive Profile

We entered the water on a high slack on the north side of the island just inside the 32 fathom mark located on NOAA chart 18421 and swam close to the island. After descending to 60 feet, we worked our way southeast around the two rocks shown on the chart. Our exit was in a shallow cove on the east side of the island.

The rock wall was heavily encrusted with sea anemones. White plumed anemones were the most common, but there were orange ones, and large green ones in the crevices. We saw cup coral, giant barnacles, and a yellowish brown hairy sea squirt. The "hairs" are made of cellulose. Red sea gherkins and pecten scallops added to the color.

It was interesting to watch the slow, ungainly swimming of the Pacific spiny lumpsucker. This small fish looks like it hasn't quite mastered water navigation. There were both brown rockfish and china rockfish. Hanging upside down in a little cave was a sailfin sculpin.

We noticed some leather sea stars and basket stars and many red and purple sea urchins. One wolfeel poked its head out of its lair and we assumed its mate was nearby. A reddish brown sea blubber with hundreds of trailing tentacles drifted by.

Directions

James Island is located 3.47 miles (270 degrees) from Shannon Point (the ramp in Washington Park) and 1.1 miles (326 degrees) from Belle Rock. You can launch your boat at Deception Pass, Flounder Bay, Washington Park, or Cap Sante in Anacortes.

James Island was named for a sailor who saved the life of U.S. naval hero Stephen Decatur. The state park there has moorage for about 10 boats. There are 3 camping areas with small beaches, for a total of 13 units, firepits, and restrooms. There is no fresh water. Many trails cross the island and you may see eagles as you explore.

Hazards

Check the rocks and current flows around the island. Thatcher Pass, between Decatur and Blakely Islands, is a favorite route for boaters either heading to or returning from the San Juan Islands. This is also a popular fishing spot so the boat traffic is always heavy.

If a wind should whip up, a short run through Thatcher Pass takes you to the more protected waters on the west side of Decatur and Blakely Islands.

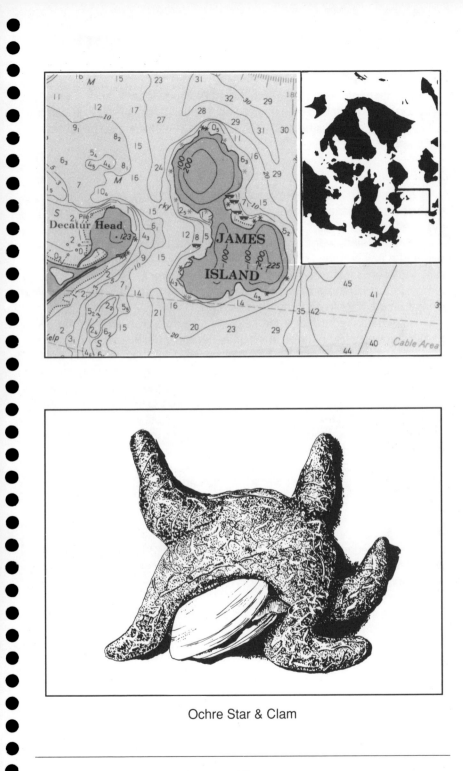

Ochre Star & Clam

Habitat and Depth

Do not confuse this dive with Kellett Bluff on Henry Island. This is a rocky region. Kellett Ledge is marked by a buoy. It has a heavy growth of bull kelp in season. Visibility is 10 to 15 feet. Great diving can be found at any depth.

Dive Profile

We entered the water on a slack ebb, headed east, and followed the ledge down to a maximum of about 60 feet. We continued around the point and headed west.

Since Kellett Ledge is exposed at low tides, the beginning of the dive revealed a few varieties of life that you do not usually see on a San Juan dive. Violet encrusting sponge covered patches of rock. There were horse barnacles among the pink-tipped and green sea anemones. We noticed several blood stars fixed beneath the ledge.

As we passed through the kelp, we saw kelp crab and shrimp. At greater depths, white plumed anemones began to dominate. There were also red sea gherkins and orange cup coral. A number of small water jellyfish floated by. Ostrich plume hydroids with 6 inch brown fronds grew in the rock clefts. We also noticed rose sea stars, green sea urchins, and red rock crab. A large lingcod swam close and we passed within inches of a painted greenling that was lying motionless against a rock.

A large octopus, probably 8 feet, was wedged into a rock crevice. We carefully took hold of a tentacle and the octopus grabbed us back. We played a gentle game of tug of war. We would give a little pull, and the octopus would tug in return. Not wishing to annoy or alarm the creature, we soon left it to its own devices.

Directions

Kellett Ledge is 2 miles NNE of Point Colville (25 degrees) and 5.47 miles NW from Deception Island (298 degrees). You can launch your boat at Deception pass, Flounder Bay, Washington Park, or Cap Sante in Anacortes.

It is a straight run north to James Island for relaxing. (See James Island dive for facilities information.)

Hazards

Do not run close to or over the ledge. Kellett Ledge extends 700 yards off Cape St. Mary. It is exposed at low tides. Be alert for fishing nets.

If the wind does kick up, it is a short run through Lopez Pass to the more protected waters of Lopez Sound.

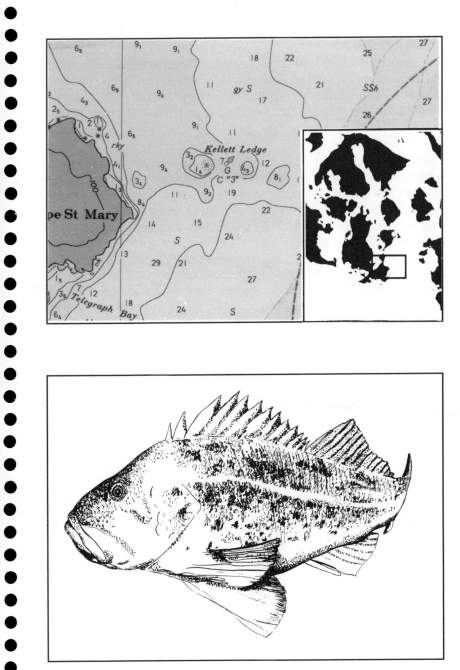

Brown Rockfish

(19) LAWSON ROCK

Habitat and Depth

Lawson Rock is located midchannel in Thatcher Pass and is marked by a day beacon. Do not confuse this dive with either Lawson Reef near Deception Pass or Lawson Bluff on Sucia Island. Visibility is 10 to 20 feet. The area has lots of kelp. You can choose your maximum depth.

Dive Profile

We dove on a high tide because it gets very shallow around the rock on a low tide and, therefore, makes a long swim for the divers to return to the boat. We entered the water near the kelp and were surprised by the number of kelp greenling and black rockfish we saw right away. There were small lingcod as well. It looks like it would be a good area for big lings, but we did not see any.

Abalone, rock scallops, large white and pink tipped anemones, and various kinds of sea urchins cling to the rock. We noticed a hermit crab and several red rock crab. There are also abundant pecten scallops. We were lucky enough to find a good sized octopus outside its home, and later ran across a pair of wolfeels.

We made sure we were always aware of our position and were careful to come up in the kelp to avoid the heavy, heavy boat traffic.

Directions

Lawson Rock is 1 mile (330 degrees) from James Island and 2.78 miles (259 degrees) from Reef Point. You can launch your boat at Deception Pass, Flounder Bay, Washington Park, Cap Sante in Anacortes, or Bellingham. If you are ferrying your boat to the islands, you can launch at Rosario, Deer Harbor, Terrill Beach, or West Beach on Orcas Island.

James Island State Park has a moorage float, a dock, and moorage buoys. There are campsites, firepits, and restrooms, and 3 small beaches. There is no fresh water. (See James Island dive for more information.)

Hazards

Be prepared for thick fog during the spring and fall. Boat traffic here is extremely heavy. You also need to watch out for large swells caused by the passing ferries.

Winds can make Rosario Strait quite rough in the afternoon. If you are on the west side of the strait, go through Peavine Pass or Thatcher Pass to the protected waters on the inside of Blakely and Decatur Islands. The east sides of Cypress and Guemes Islands will provide you with enough wind protection to allow for a safe run back to Anacortes.

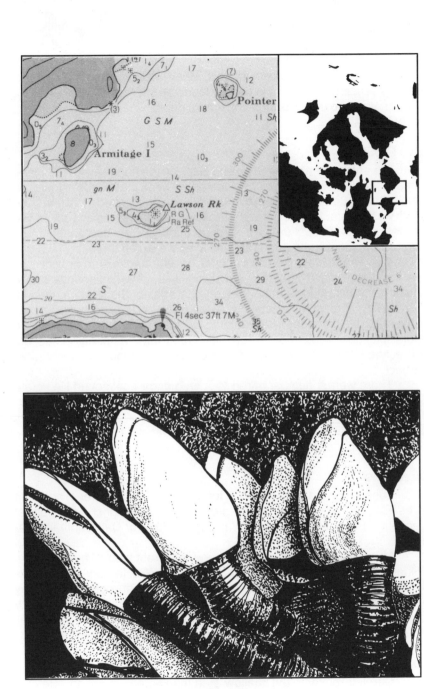

Goose-neck Barnacles

Habitat and Depth

The habitat is rocky with ledges. Heavy kelp is present during the growing season. Good diving can be found as shallow as 10 ft. or as deep as your most comfortable maximum depth. Visibility ranges from 20 to 30 feet.

Dive Profile

We entered the water on an ebb slack on the north side of the island at the most northern point which is located between the two rocks found on NOAA Chart 18421. We swam to the rocks and descended to 10 feet. Our depth was constantly changing as we followed the ledges up and down. We headed south and east until we reached the thick kelp bed on the south side. It was too thick to penetrate easily so we exited there.

If you appreciate the rich varieties of color and texture provided by sea life, Long Island is a very satisfying dive. The solid white of the anemones contrasted with the feathery tentacles of the red sea gherkin. The purple and giant red sea urchins were sharp and spiked; the branches of the staghorn bryozoa were blunt and rounded. Tiny cup coral provided bright splashes of color. Giant sea cucumbers were rather dull in hue, but interesting in texture. We noted a large cloud sponge and many giant barnacles.

There were a number of red rock crab and Puget sound king crab. Several pink and gray-striped sun stars, a leather star, and the bright orange-red vermilion star were visible. A few rock scallops, some abalone, and many pecten scallops were also there. Swimming residents included kelp greenling, copper rockfish, and great sculpin.

Directions

Long Island is 1.5 miles NW of Iceberg Point (318 degrees) and 1.34 miles East of Cattle Point (112 degrees). You can launch your boat at Deception Pass, Flounder Bay, Washington Park, or Cap Sante in Anacortes.

MacKaye Harbor offers anchorage for a rest stop. The San Juan Wilderness, administered by the U.S. Fish and Wildlife Service, includes over twenty rocks and tiny islands off the southern tip of Lopez Island. They have been set aside for wildlife management and are home to a wide variety of sea birds. If you are interested in birdlife, bring binoculars and stay well clear of the islands so the birds are not disturbed.

Hazards

Carefully observe the shallow area marked on your chart. Be alert for fishing nets. If the wind comes up, see Colville Island dive for shelter information.

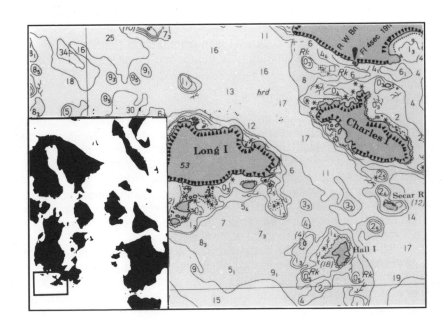

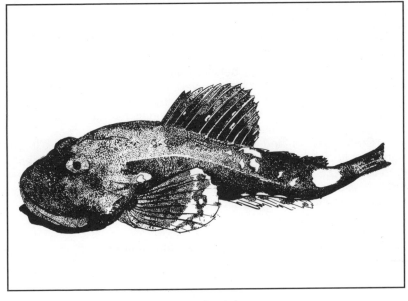

Great Sculpin

Habitat and Depth

Lopez Pass has a rock wall with a mud/sand bottom. Maximum depth is 84 feet. Kelp is located near the rocks. Visibility varies from 7 to 10 feet.

Dive Profile

We entered the water on a low ebb just in front of the light at the south end of Decatur Island and shown on NOAA chart 18421. We descended close to the wall to avoid boat traffic and eventually reached about 80 feet. Taking a compass heading, we crossed the muddy/sandy bottom of the Pass and exited just inside the kelp on the Lopez side.

The descent down the wall had all the color and beauty you would expect on a San Juan wall dive. Pecten and rock scallops abounded. Sunflower stars, rose stars, white and green anemones, green, purple, and giant red sea urchins all made a colorful display.

When we reached the bottom of the wall, the habitat changed to mud. As we crossed the pass, we found both Dungeness and red rock crab. We ascended just inside the kelp on the Lopez side to be sure we avoided the boat traffic in this narrow pass. In the kelp we saw graceful kelp crab and kelp greenling.

Directions

Lopez Pass is located off the southern tip of Decatur Island and is 5.73 miles (252) from Shannon Point (the ramp at Washington Park). You can launch your boat at Deception Pass, Flounder Bay, Washington Park, or Cap Sante in Anacortes.

Lopez Island, Pass, and Sound are named in honor of Lopez Gonzales de Haro who many believe was the real discoverer of the San Juan Islands. Haro Strait is also derived from his rather long name.

A short run up the east side of Decatur Island takes you to James Island State Park. There are campsites, firepits, restrooms, and boat moorage. (See James Island dive.)

Crab, Fortress, and Skull Islands (actually more like rocks than islands) in Lopez Sound between Hunter Bay and Mud Bay are managed by the U.S. Fish and Wildlife Service as part of the San Juan Wilderness. You can often observe several varieties of seabirds here, but be sure to stay well clear. Seals frequently haul out here as well.

Hazards

The pass has a depth of 9 to 12 fathoms but is very narrow. The northeastern entrance is guarded by a reef which creates Rim, Rum, and Ram Islands. Listen carefully for boat traffic as you ascend.

If the wind becomes too strong, you can continue west into the more protected waters of Lopez Sound.

Grunt Sculpin

Habitat and Depth

Whale Rocks consist of rocky walls with kelp present in the growing season. You can choose your maximum depth. Visibility is 20 to 30 feet.

Dive Profile

We entered the water on a slack ebb just on the north side of the rocks located on NOAA chart 18421. This is an exciting, high current area which drains the whole San Juan Channel. We gradually descended to a maximum of 60 feet, always listening for boat engines as this is an area of heavy boat traffic. We swam around the rocks, exploring as we went. It is important to remain conscious of the current pressure so that the turn of the tide does not catch you unaware.

The rocks are covered with an abundance of underwater life. White and pink-tipped anemones grow in thick clusters. Abalone, rock scallops, and giant red sea urchins cling here too. Pecten scallops flit about. Cup coral and the orange-red tentacles of the red sea gherkins caught the eye, as did a bright orange vermilion star. We saw Puget Sound king crab and quite a few red rock crab. We discovered brown, quillback, and china rockfish. There were also kelp greenling and cabezon.

Directions

Whale Rocks is located 0.6 of a mile north of Long Island (309 degrees) and 0.9 of a mile (100 degrees) east of Cattle Point. You can launch your boat at Deception Pass, Flounder Bay, Washington Park, or Cap Sante in Anacortes.

MacKaye Harbor offers anchorage for a lunch stop. Or you can cross San Juan Channel to Griffin Bay. (See Colville Island dive.)

If you are interested in birdlife, you may want to take a look at some of the sanctuaries managed by the U.S. Fish and Wildlife Service. Nearby are Shark Reef, Mummy Rocks near Davis Bay, Secar Rock, and Hall Island, southeast of Long Island. Many types of birds either nest here or stop on their migrations. Use binoculars from a distance to look at the birds since they are easily frightened.

Hazards

The rocks are hidden during high tide. Remember this is an area of high currents and frequent winds. If the winds become a problem, see Colville Island dive for shelter information. It is also a fairly short run through San Juan Channel to Friday Harbor or east to Fisherman Bay on Lopez Island.

Boat traffic is heavy. Fishermen may also present a problem.

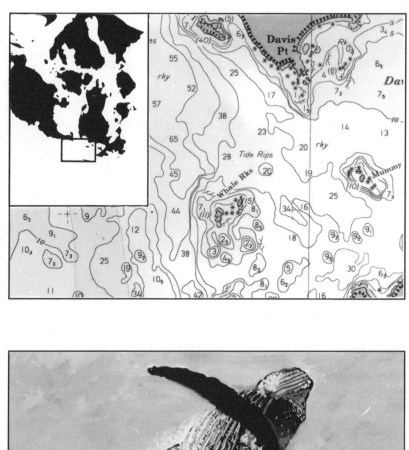

Humpback Whale

(23) BATTLESHIP ISLAND

Habitat and Depth

Battleship Island is located just to the northwest of Henry Island. It is a rocky habitat with many large boulders. Visibility is 15 to 25 feet and a comfortable diving depth is about 60 feet. Kelp is present.

Dive Profile

Our point of entry was the southeast corner of the island, facing McCracken Point as shown on NOAA chart 18421. We dove the tail end of a flood tide and descended just in front of the kelp. The current carried us NNW. Battleship Island is narrow from east to west and water depth increases quickly on the north and west sides. The current is strong but you can duck behind the many large boulders to get out of it.

The high current accounts for the abundance of life that covers the rocks. The white plumed and pink tipped anemones vie with red and green sea urchins. Violet encrusting sponge mingles with cup coral, sea lettuce and yellowish dead man's fingers. Kelp crab, red rock crab, and many pecten scallops inhabit the area.

Between the rocks we glimpsed lingcod. Rockfish schooled about, and there were also some kelp greenling.

Directions

Battleship Island is located about 0.2 of a mile WNW (319 degrees) off McCracken Point on Henry Island and 1.69 miles (211 degrees) from the west tip of Spieden Island. You can launch your boat at Deception Pass, Flounder Bay, Washington Park, or Cap Sante in Anacortes. If you are driving to the Islands, you can launch at Roche Harbor Boatel, Snug Harbor Marina, or San Juan County Park, all on San Juan Island; or you can launch at Rosario, Deer Harbor, Terrill Beach, or West Beach on Orcas Island.

There are several small beaches on Henry Island, but only the tidelands are public. San Juan County Park at Smallpox Bay on San Juan Island has picnic facilities and limited moorage. (See Bellevue Point dive.)

Battleship Island is one of the eighty-four islands belonging to the San Juan Island Wilderness Area. Going ashore is prohibited in order to protect the seabirds who use these islands as nesting areas. Look at Battleship Island in profile and you will see how it got its name.

Hazards

Be extremely cautious around Danger Shoal, Center Reef, Barren Island, and a rock 200 yards north of Barren Island. The entrance to Spieden Channel is risky in low visibility.

Winds can make Haro strait quite rough in the afternoon. A short run back to Roche Harbor or Snug Harbor will provide you with good anchorage, modern facilities, and plenty of protection from a storm.

This is a high current area so exercise caution.

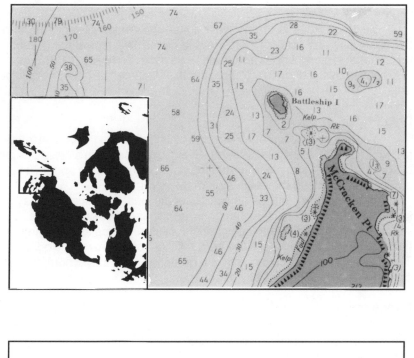

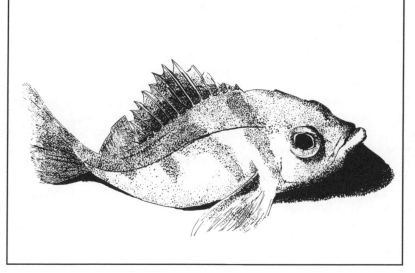

Splitnose Rockfish

Habitat and Depth

Bellevue Point is on the west coast of San Juan Island, south of Smallpox Bay and north of the Lime Kiln Light. This typical rocky habitat has gradual to steep slopes and some large rocks. Visibility is 20 to 30 feet. You can choose your own maximum depth. There can be heavy kelp in the area.

Dive Profile

We entered the water on the slack, just in front of the point itself, as shown on NOAA chart 18421. First we explored the north side at a depth of about 40 feet. Later, we rounded the point, went down to about 60 feet, and continued diving the south side of the point.

Many pecten scallops as well as occasional rock scallops may be seen here. Cup coral, white anemones, and sponge live on the rocks. You will spot the tentacles of red sea gherkins capturing food and bringing it to their mouths. Lots of rockfish live here. We identified brown and quillback. There are also great sculpin and kelp greenling. We saw a northern kelp crab, red rock crab, and a shy octopus.

Directions

Bellevue Point is located 0.7 of a mile south of Smallpox Bay. You can launch your boat at Deception Pass, Flounder Bay, Washington Park, or Cap Sante in Anacortes. If you are driving to the Islands, you can launch at Roche Harbor Boatel, Snug Harbor Marina, or San Juan County Park, all on San Juan Island; or you can launch at Rosario, Deer Harbor, Terrill Beach, or West Beach on Orcas Island.

Smallpox Bay was named when some Native Americans who contracted the disease tried to lessen the fever by jumping into the waters of the bay. It is home to San Juan County Park, the only campground on San Juan Island. There are fifteen acres with eleven campsites, restrooms, a boat launch, moorage for two boats, but no drinking water.

Diving at the park and at nearby Low Island is very popular. As you would expect, the campground is often full. The best time to come here is in the off-season or on weekdays if you must come during the summer.

Sighting killer whales is always a possibility. One of the favorite summer feeding areas ranges between Smallpox Bay and American Camp to the south. Bellevue Point derives its name from the early British name for San Juan Island.

Hazards

Winds can make Haro Strait quite rough in the afternoon. Smallpox Bay is open on the west and is shallow. (See Battleship Island dive for shelter information.)

Bald Eagle

Habitat and Depth

Center Reef bares at low tide. This reef dive is for experienced divers only. The reef is marked by a buoy on its southwest side. Maximum depth is unlimited. Visibility ranges from 20 to 45 feet. Kelp is present in the growing season.

Dive Profile

We entered the water north of the buoy. The top of the reef looks almost windswept by the heavy currents, but the deep cracks and crevices are full of life. You will find white and pink tipped anemones, red and purple sea urchins, red sea gherkins, encrusting sponge, rock scallops, and crab. We noticed copper, quillback, and black rockfish, cabezon, greenling, and small lingcod.

There are many pieces of lost fishing gear and quite a few anchors. If you anchor here, don't plan on getting it back unless you dive for it.

Directions

Center Reef is 0.47 of a mile (240) degrees from Sentinel Island and 0.95 miles (57) degrees from Battleship Island. You can launch your boat at Deception Pass, Flounder Bay, Washington Park, or Cap Sante in Anacortes. If you are ferrying your boat to the Islands, you can launch at Roche Harbor Boatel, Snug Harbor Marina, or San Juan County Park, all on San Juan Island; or you can launch at Rosario, Deer Harbor, Terrill Beach, or West Beach on Orcas Island.

Center Reef and nearby Sentinel Rock are part of the San Juan Islands Wilderness bird refuges.

It is not a long run to Stuart Island State Park. There are 19 campsites, firepits, water and moorage for 48 boats. (See Turn Point dive for more information.)

Hazards

During spring and fall, fog can be heavy. Winds can make Spieden Channel quite rough in the afternoon. Roche Harbor provides good shelter and facilities.

The current is extremely swift here, making this dive unsuitable for a novice and only safe when done from a live boat. It is a good idea to carry a compass because the reef is much bigger underwater than it looks on the charts. A depth sounder will make it easier to locate the reef.

There is a lot of boat traffic here, especially in the summer.

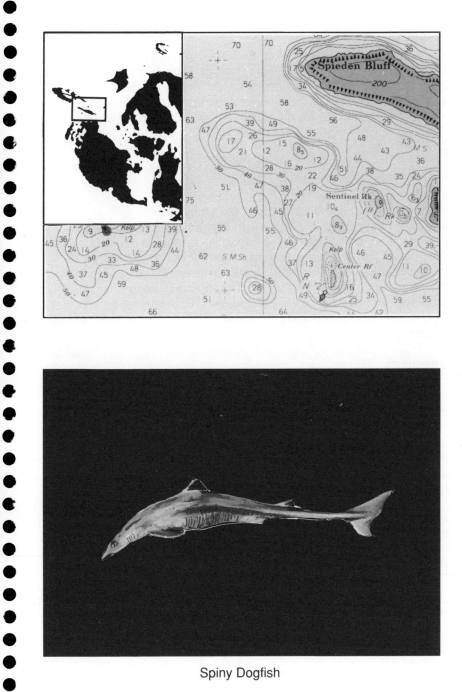

Spiny Dogfish

Habitat and Depth

Charles Point is located on the northern shore of Stuart Island. It is at the western entrance to Prevost Harbor. This rocky habitat has both large and small boulders with sandy gravel areas from time to time. There is kelp along the wall. A good dive can be had in as shallow as 20 feet of water, or down to your maximum depth. Visibility is 20 to 30 feet.

Dive Profile

Charles Point is an excellent choice if you are in the area on a full flood. Diving along the wall on the north side of Stuart Island, you are afforded good protection from the full force of the current. We entered the water just in front of the rock which marks the entrance to Prevost Harbor and swam west. We dove the area in the morning so we did not have the advantage of full sunlight. It is advisable to dive as late in the day as possible: If you dive early, you may need to take a light with you.

We saw swarms of small fish staying next to shore and in and around the kelp beds. There were also cabezon, many kinds of rockfish, kelp greenling, and lingcod, as we went deeper. The rocks held white anemones, sea pumpkins, red and purple sea urchins, rock scallops, and a few abalone.

Directions

Charles Point is located just east of Turn Point on Stuart Island. It is 1.30 miles (92 degrees) from Turn Point and 6.47 miles (277 degrees) from Point Disney on Waldron Island. You can launch your boat at Deception Pass, Flounder Bay, Washington Park, or Cap Sante in Anacortes. If you are driving to the islands, you can launch at Roche Harbor Boatel, Snug Harbor Marina, or San Juan County Park, all on San Juan Island; or you can launch at Rosario, Deer Harbor, Terrill Beach, or West Beach on Orcas Island.

Stuart Island State Park takes up 152 acres and includes both Reid and Prevost Harbors. It has moorage for 48 boats, 19 campsites with firepits, restrooms, and water. (See Turn Point dive for more information.)

Hazards

Plan on thick fog here during the spring and fall. Winds can make President Channel and Boundary Pass quite rough in the afternoon. Currents on an ebb tide can exceed 6 knots. Deer Harbor, Roche Harbor, West Bound and Friday Harbor are all within easy reach. Prevost Harbor, north side of Stuart Island, and Reid Harbor, southeast side of Stuart Island, both provide good shelter and anchorage. Be aware of submerged rocks and shoals at the entrance to Reid Harbor. A shoal also extends eastward from Stuart Island at the south entrance to Johns Pass.

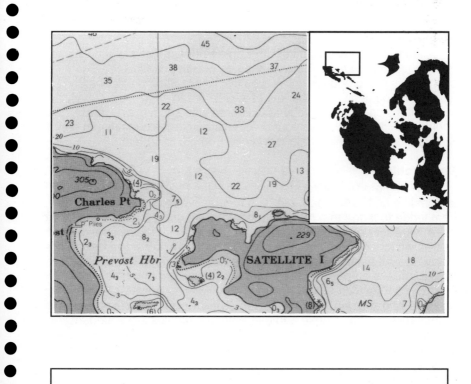

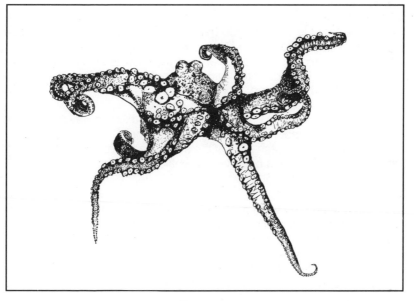

Octopus

㉗ EAGLE POINT, San Juan Island

Habitat and Depth

Do not confuse this dive with Eagle Point on Matia Island. Eagle Point is located on the southwestern side of San Juan Island. The shoreline is steep and rocky. Waves from Haro Strait break sharply against the point giving it the feel of a wild, ocean shore. Underwater, the habitat slopes quickly to ledges littered with sand, gravel, and boulders. You can choose your own most comfortable maximum depth. Kelp is along the bank. Visibility ranges from 20 to 40 feet.

Dive Profile

We entered the water just off the tip of the Point and inside the eleven fathom line on NOAA chart 18421. Our plan was to make our way down from ledge to ledge to a maximum depth of around 75 feet. We'd heard there were lots of octopuses here, and we weren't disappointed. Altogether, we found three, the largest about four and a half or five feet across. Many types of anemones cover the rocks and give bright splashes of white and green and orange. Between the anemones are barnacles, staghorn bryozoa, and ostrich plume hydroid. You will find pecten scallops, rock scallops, and abalone here. Wolfeels hide in the crevices. We saw red rock crab and kelp crab. Purple and giant red sea urchins are abundant.

This area is home to many fish. You will see all types of rockfish, kelp greenling, and cabezon. On our dive we noticed goodsized lingcod.

Directions

Eagle Point is 3 miles (280 degrees) NW of Cattle Point. You can launch your boat at Deception Pass, Flounder Bay, Washington Park, or Cap Sante in Anacortes. If you are ferrying your boat to the Islands, you can launch at Roche Harbor Boatel, Snug Harbor Marina, or San Juan County Park, all on San Juan Island; or you can launch at Rosario, Deer Harbor, Terrill Beach, or West Beach on Orcas Island.

Eagle Cove County Park on Haro Strait and Griffin Bay on San Juan Channel have moorage available for a lunch stop.

You will always catch sight of the eagles that give the Point its name. Quite often you will see a pod of killer whales that frequents this area.

Hazards

Avoid letting the wind push you in too close to the point itself. It is deep just off the point and the tendency is to become a little careless with the wind while concentrating on depth.

Heavy swells are always a possibility, and the weather can change very quickly in the winter months. Mackaye Harbor on Lopez offers protected anchorage in 25 to 30 feet of water. Fisherman Bay and Friday Harbor on San Juan also offer protection from the storms.

Be alert for kelp, strong currents, and boat traffic. There are many commercial fishing vessels in the area during the season.

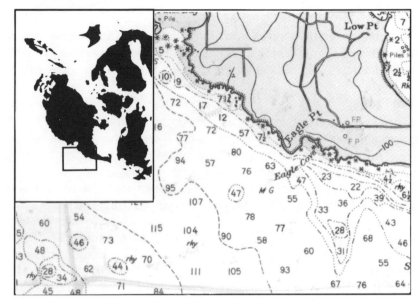

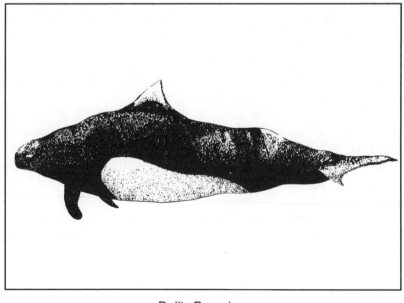

Dall's Porpoise

(28) JOHNS ISLAND

Habitat and Depth

Johns Island lies northwest of San Juan Island. This is a steep, rocky area with small caves and fissures in the rock. You can choose your own maximum depth. Visibility ranges from 20 to 40 feet. Kelp is present.

Dive Profile

We chose to dive from the SE point on the outside, just inside the 15 fathom line on the north side of the island, entering the water on an ebb slack tide. We descended to 60 feet and drifted in a NW direction, finishing our dive 30 minutes later and 200 feet from our entry point.

Octopuses like the little cracks in the rock here. One we saw was about 8 feet. There are probably wolfeels, but we didn't see any.

A large brownish sea blubber, maybe 2 to 3 feet, floated past with tentacles trailing. Abalone and rock scallops adhere to the rocks. There were a number of basket stars, pecten scallops, and some Puget Sound king crab. We found brown and quillback rockfish, kelp greenling, and some good-sized lingcod.

Directions

Johns Island is located 3.52 miles (227 degrees) from Sandy Point, Waldron Island, and 2.7 miles (260 degrees) from White Rocks. You can launch your boat at Deception Pass, Flounder Bay, Washington Park, or Cap Sante in Anacortes. If you are driving to the Islands, you can launch at Roche Harbor Boatel, Snug Harbor Marina, or San Juan County Park, all on San Juan Island; or you can launch at Rosario, Deer Harbor, Terrill Beach, or West Beach on Orcas Island.

The beaches around Johns Island are pea gravel, and only the tidelands are public. Stuart Island State Park to the west has campsites with firepit, restrooms, and drinking water. Boat moorage is available at Prevost Harbor and Reid Harbor. (See Turn Point dive.)

Hazards

You will frequently run into heavy fog during the spring and fall. Be prepared for strong winds that can make President Channel and San Juan Channel rough in the afternoon. (See Charles Point dive for shelter information.)

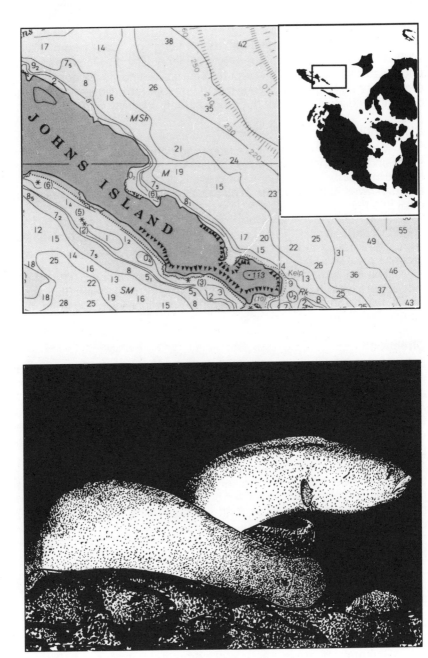

Penpoint Gunnel

(29) KELLETT BLUFF

Habitat and Depth

Do not confuse this dive with Kellett Ledge on Lopez Island. Kellett Bluff is located near the southern end of Henry Island which is part of an underwater shelf. This is a steep, rocky area with no visible beach. Kelp grows right up to the wall. Your maximum depth is unlimited as the wall drops immediately down for hundreds of feet. Visibility is 20 to 45 feet.

Dive Profile

We entered the water on a slack tide right in front of the light at the south end of Henry Island, located on NOAA chart 18425, and drifted east toward the point. The unique features of this dive are the many large cracks and big caves to be explored. You must have a light as the caves go far back into the wall.

Anemones are everywhere, as well as purple sea urchins, red sea gherkins, and cup coral. We saw several varieties of crab and some basket stars. We ran into perch, china rockfish, copper rockfish, and kelp greenling.

The real attractions here though are the huge lingcod. They like to hide in the caves. If you miss them the first time, do dive Kellett Bluff again. About half the time we dive here, we run across lings weighing better than thirty-five pounds.

Directions

Kellett Bluff is located 3.17 miles (332 degrees) from Smallpox Bay and 1.08 miles (297) degrees from Hanbury Pt. You can launch your boat at Deception Pass, Flounder Bay, Washington Park, or Cap Sante in Anacortes. If you are ferrying your boat to the islands, you can launch at Roche Harbor Boatel, Snug Harbor Marina, or San Juan County Park, all on San Juan Island; or you can launch at Rosario, Deer Harbor, Terrill Beach, or West Beach on Orcas Island.

Henry Island itself is privately owned, but the tidelands of the tiny beaches at Kellett Bluff, McCracken Point, and Henry Island Beach are public. None is protected, so you are better off anchoring in one of the many coves for a lunch stop. Kellett Bluff takes its name from a British naval captain who charted the area.

Hazards

Don't let the wind blow you into the island while dropping off or picking up divers. Fog can be a hazard during the fall diving season. Kelp is heavy so carry a knife.

Winds can make Haro Strait quite rough in the afternoon. Roche Harbor offers protected anchorage. Open Bay, east of Kellett Bluff, gives shelter from the north and east.

Remember that this is an area of extremely strong currents. They run very fast in both directions, and you cannot swim against them. You must have a live boat to make this dive.

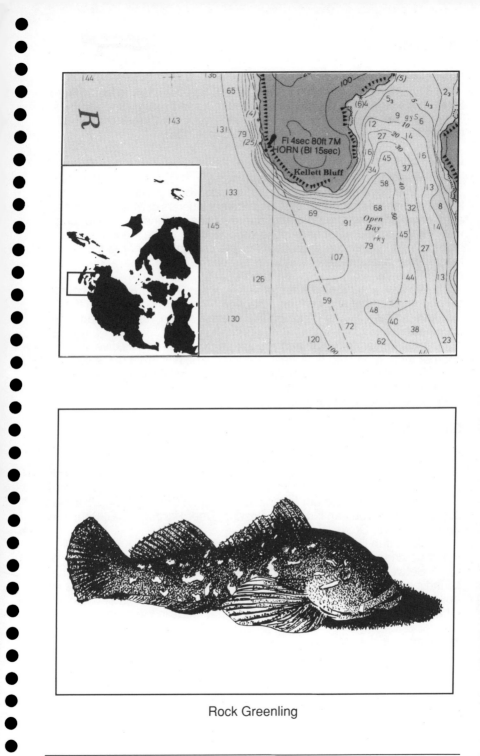

Rock Greenling

Habitat and Depth

Lime Kiln is located on the west side of San Juan Island facing Haro Strait. It is an area of rocky ledges covered with sand, gravel, and boulders. There is a lot of kelp here. You can pick your own most comfortable maximum depth. Visibility ranges from 20 to 40 feet.

Dive Profile

We entered the water just in front of the light located on NOAA chart 18421. We dove below the kelp and began working our way down the ledges to a depth of about 80 feet. There were clusters of white plumed sea anemones and lots of purple and giant red sea urchins. Abalone, dead man's fingers, and violet encrusting sponge clung to the ledges. Several types of rockfish schooled about. Red sea cucumbers shared the sandy ledges with beautiful pink nudibranchs and vermilion stars added more color.

We saw a number of kelp greenling, a small octopus, and a couple of lingcod. A pair of shy wolfeels inhabited a large crevice at about the 40 foot level. Water jellyfish, looking like strange space vehicles, appeared from nowhere.

If the current picks up and you are unable to make this dive, there is another more protected dive west, around the point in front of the old lime kilns. It is away from the traffic and current, and while it lacks the variety of life of the point dive, it is still interesting. Large pillars and machinery from the lime kiln days litter the bottom.

Directions

Lime Kiln is located 1.52 miles (167 degrees) from Smallpox Bay and 3.13 miles (312 degrees) from Pile Point. You can launch your boat at Deception Pass, Flounder Bay, Washington Park, or Cap Sante in Anacortes. If you are ferrying your boat to the islands, you can launch at Roche Harbor Boatel, Snug Harbor Marina, or San Juan County Park, all on San Juan Island; or you can launch at Rosario, Deer Harbor, Terrill Beach, or West Beach on Orcas Island.

San Juan County Park at Smallpox Bay is close by and has limited moorage and picnic facilities for a lunch stop. (See Bellevue Point dive.)

Between dives there is plenty to explore at this site of one of San Juan Island's earliest lime kilns. There are excavations and remnants of the old buildings, wells, and machines. The view from the cliffs is spectacular. Often you will see a pod of killer whales that feeds in the area.

Hazards

Be alert for an easterly wind which can push your boat into the island while unloading or loading divers. Winds can make Haro Strait quite rough in the afternoon. There is no shelter at the point and heavy winter swells and fast-changing weather patterns can cause problems. (See Battleship Island dive for shelter information.)

In addition to current and kelp, be alert for boat traffic and commercial fishing operations during the season. You may see killer whales.

Bonaparte's Gull

LOW ISLAND

Habitat and Depth

There are two Low Islands in the San Juans. This one is on the west side of San Juan Island, just opposite Small Pox Bay and San Juan County Park. It is half-moon shaped and rocky, with ledges and interesting cracks and holes. You can choose your own maximum depth. Visibility ranges from 25 to 40 feet. There is lots of kelp during the growing season.

Dive Profile

We entered the water on the northwest corner of Low Island on a high slack. We descended to 60 feet and swam in a southerly direction on the outside of the island. We then increased our depth to 80 feet and gradually worked our way up to the kelp in 30 feet of water.

This is a great place to take pictures because of the good visibility and the colorful variety of life. White anemones, rock scallops, red and green sea urchins, and abalone cling to the rocks. There are both octopuses and wolfeels hiding in the holes. You will see a lot of fish including greenling, cabezon, all varieties of rockfish, bass, and lingcod.

The current on the shore side is moderate, but along the western side, it really moves. Don't attempt to dive it without a live boat.

Directions

Low Island is 3.26 miles (153 degrees) from the marker on Kellett Bluff and just north of Bellevue Point. You can launch your boat at Deception pass, Flounder Bay, Washington Park, or Cap Sante in Anacortes. If you are driving to the islands, you can launch at Rosario, Deer Harbor, Terrill Beach, or West Beach, all on Orcas Island; or you can launch at Roche Harbor and Snug Harbor on San Juan Island.

Low Island is part of the San Juan Wilderness Area. No one is allowed ashore in order to protect the nesting seabirds. San Juan County Park, opposite Low Island, has campsites, restrooms, and limited boat moorage. Because it is the only public camping facility on San Juan Island, it is usually filled to capacity during the summer and on weekends. Try this dive in the off-season. (See Bellevue Point dive.)

Hazards

You may find heavy fog during the spring and fall. Winds can make Haro Strait quite rough in the afternoon. Friday Harbor, Snug Harbor, and Roche Harbor have marine supplies and assistance.

Do not attempt this dive as a shore dive. It is just far enough from shore to make the swim dangerous. Also be alert for pods of killer whales when you are on the surface. This is part of their habitual range.

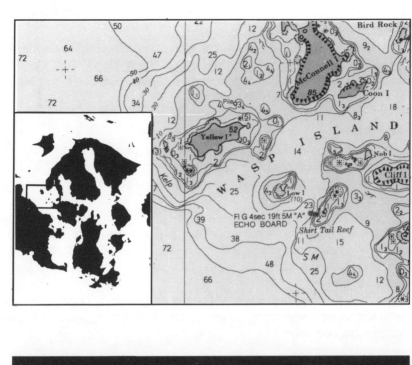

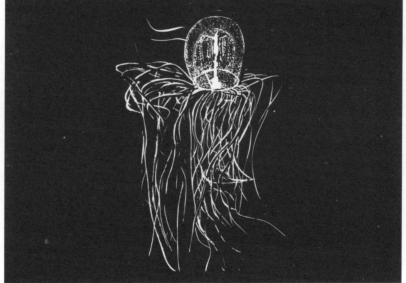

Pencillate Jellyfish

③② McCRACKEN POINT

Habitat and Depth

Here you actually are diving the kelp covered reef that extends out from McCracken Point on the northwest tip of Henry Island. This is a good shallow dive to cap off a day of deeper diving. Maximum depth is about 30 feet. Visibility ranges from 30 to 40 feet.

Dive Profile

Diving the end of a rising tide, we entered the water next to the kelp on the southwest corner of McCracken Point as shown on NOAA chart 18421. We drifted over the reef and then dropped below it to the sand and gravel on the northern side.

The reef rocks carried the usual carpet of giant white plumed and green anemones sprinkled with encrusting bryozoa, cup coral, and red sea urchins. We saw glassy sea squirts, red sea gherkins, pecten scallops, sun stars, and sunflower stars. We were lucky enough to see many different varieties of rockfish.

When we dove below the reef on the north side, we found a sandy, gravel habitat with kelp crab, red sea cucumbers, lemon peel and striped nudibranchs, and flounder.

Directions

McCracken Point, on Henry Island, is located 1 mile (223 degrees) from Center Reef and 0.2 miles (137 degrees) from Battleship Island. You can launch your boat at Deception Pass, Flounder Bay, Washington Park, or Cap Sante in Anacortes. If you are driving to the islands, you can launch at Roche Harbor Boatel, Snug Harbor Marina, or San Juan County Park, all on San Juan Island; or you can launch at Rosario, Deer Harbor, Terrill Beach, or West Beach on Orcas Island.

Henry Island itself is privately owned, but the tidelands at McCracken Point, Kellett Bluff, and Henry Island Beach are public. The beaches are tiny, gravelly, and unprotected. You are probably wise to anchor in one of the many small bays or coves to make your lunch stop.

Hazards

Be watchful of shoals, rocks, and kelp. Fog can present its own problems during the fall diving season.

Winds can make Haro Strait quite rough in the afternoon. Snug Harbor or Roche Harbor offer excellent protection during a storm.

Rock Scallop

Habitat Depth

Pile Point lies northwest of False Bay on the west coast of San Juan Island. It is an extremely rocky area with vertical walls, ledges, and large boulders. On the south side there is gravel formed by rockslides. You can choose your own maximum depth. Visibility ranges from 30 to 40 feet. Kelp lies along the shoreline.

Dive Profile

We entered the water just in front of the kelp on the south side of Pile Point as shown on NOAA chart 18421. Descending between 40 and 50 feet, we drifted west on a rising tide.

Hiding in the kelp were northern kelp crab and graceful kelp crab. The rocks here are perfect homes for wolfeels who feed on the abundant pecten scallops. Rock scallops and abalone cling to the rocks. We saw some colorful seastars: a rose star, blood star, and a vermilion.

Many fish favor this area. A number of lingcod inhabit the little caves, as well as many brown rockfish and china rockfish. Some greenling live here as well. Red sea cucumbers choose the gravel covered ledges and octopuses hide in the crevices. There is a wide range of colorful life here.

Directions

Pile Point is located 2.73 miles (302 degrees) from Eagle Point and 3.13 miles (131 degrees) from Lime Kiln. You can launch your boat at Deception Pass, Flounder Bay, Washington Park, or Cap Sante in Anacortes. If you are driving to the islands, you can launch at Roche Harbor Boatel, Snug Harbor Marina, or San Juan County Park, all on San Juan Island; or you can launch at Rosario, Deer Harbor, Terrill Beach, or West Beach on Orcas Island.

San Juan County Park at Smallpox Bay has limited moorage and there are picnic facilities for a lunch stop (see Bellevue Point dive.) It is always possible to see a pod of killer whales whose summer feeding area ranges from Smallpox Bay south to American Camp.

Hazards

Be on the watch for the wind or current moving your boat into the rocks during loading or unloading of divers. All points around the island are popular fishing areas so be alert for much boat traffic.

Winds can make Haro Strait quite rough in the afternoon. Mackaye Harbor on Lopez and Roche Harbor or Snug Harbor on San Juan offer good protection from a sudden storm.

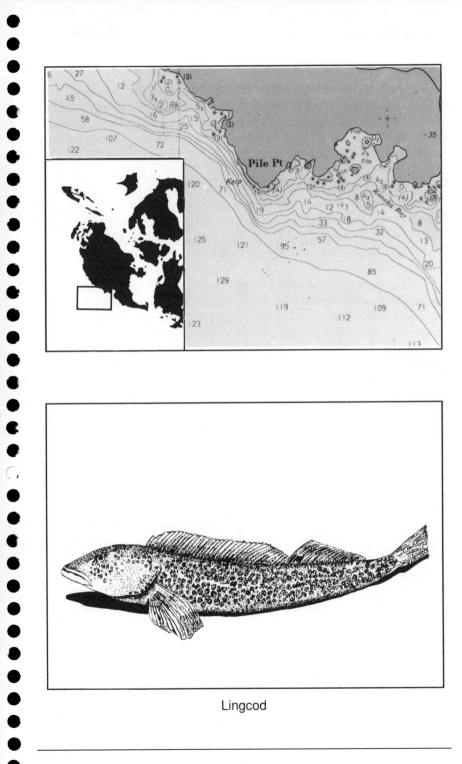

Lingcod

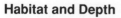

Habitat and Depth

Spieden Bluff is the most westerly point of Spieden Island, just north of San Juan Island. Typical of this area, its underwater habitat consists of large boulders, ledges, and vertical walls. There is kelp along the shore's edge. Depth can range from 20 feet to your maximum comfortable level. Visibility is 20 to 30 feet.

Dive Profile

We entered the water on the tail end of a falling tide on the west end and south side of the bluff (just north of the 55 fathom mark shown on NOAA chart 18421). From that point we swam 100 feet west toward the point in 20-40 feet of water. Later we descended to 60 feet and swam back toward the southeast.

There are many places for fish to hide out. We ran across brown, copper, and quillback rockfish, small lingcod, and kelp greenling.

The rocks were colorfully covered with white and green anemones, purple and green sea urchins, cushion stars, feather dusters, and rock scallops. We found kelp crab and pecten scallops and a few abalone shells. It appeared that seals had found the abalone first.

Directions

Spieden Bluff is located at the northwest end of Spieden Island. Spieden Island lies just north of San Juan Island and just south of Johns Island. Spieden Bluff is 0.73 of a mile (360 degrees) from Center Reef and 1.65 miles (34 degrees) from Battleship Island. You can launch your boat at Deception Pass, Flounder Bay, Washington Park, or Cap Sante in Anacortes. If you are driving to the islands, you can launch at Roche Harbor Boatel, Snug Harbor Marina, or San Juan County Park, all on San Juan Island; or at Rosario, Deer Harbor, Terrill Beach, or West Beach on Orcas Island.

Spieden Island, named for a member of the Wilkes Expedition, has the distinction of being the only one of the larger San Juans not to have a bay or harbor. Only the rocky tidelands are publicly owned. One of the many coves around San Juan Island is a better bet for a lunch stop.

Hazards

There is a good possibility of heavy fog during the spring and fall. There are strong tidal currents and shoals in Spieden Channel. Winds can make Haro Strait quite rough in the afternoon. (If you need to shelter, see Charles Point dive for information.)

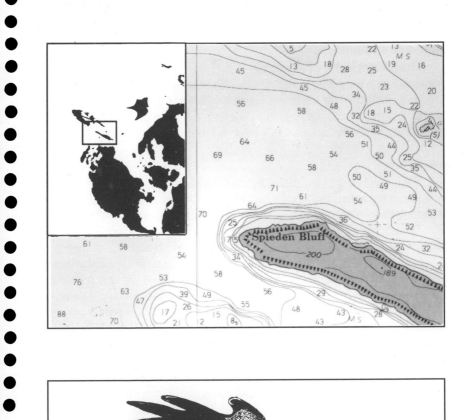

White Bellied Sea-Eagle

Habitat and Depth

Turn Point is the most northwesterly tip of Stuart Island. It is a wild, rocky area with dense kelp along the walls of the point and on the reef that extends outward. The habitat is basically rocky, but there is a mixture of sand and gravel on the reef. Diving depth is a matter of choice and of tide conditions. Visibility ranges from 20 to 30 feet.

Dive Profile

Our dive began on the north side of the Turn Point Lighthouse. Because of the extreme thickness of the kelp canopy, we chose not to swim through it and entered just in front of the kelp on the north side of the reef.

The currents here are very strong, providing food sources to feed a variety of life. The rocks held large concentrations of yellowish dead man's fingers and what we believe was cloud sponge. There were ostrich plume hydroid and encrusting bryozoa. The sea urchins were red and green; the anemones were white. Pecten scallops were abundant.

We saw brown and quillback rockfish and some kelp greenling and cabezon. When we went deeper, we found lingcod of average size.

Directions

Turn Point is located on the NW point of land on Stuart Island. Stuart Island is west of Johns Island and Spieden Island. Turn Point is 8.43 miles (252 degrees) from Skipjack Island and 4.43 miles (332 degrees) from Battleship Island. You can launch your boat at Deception Pass, Flounder Bay, Washington Park, or Cap Sante in Anacortes. If you are driving to the islands, you can launch at Roche Harbor Boatel, Snug Harbor Marina, or San Juan County Park, all on San Juan Island; or at Rosario, Deer Harbor, Terrill Beach, or West Beach on Orcas Island.

Only the tidelands are public on most of Stuart Island's beaches. However, there is a State Park located between Reid Harbor and Prevost Harbor. It has campsites with firepits, restrooms, drinking water, and moorage available. There are a number of hiking trails, including one about two and a half miles long which takes you to the Turn Point lighthouse. There you get a wonderful view across Haro Strait to the Canadian Gulf Islands and Vancouver Island beyond.

Hazards

Spring and fall can produce heavy fog. Haro Strait can get very rough in the afternoon. (See Charles Point dive for shelter information.)

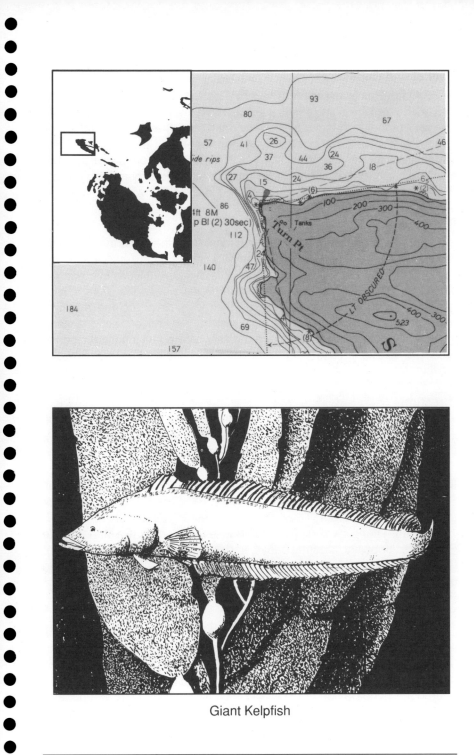

Giant Kelpfish

Habitat and Depth

Alden Point, the western tip of Patos Island, is marked by a lighthouse. East of the point, this is a typical rocky habitat for the first 30 to 40 feet. It gradually changes to gravelly sand, and then becomes a sandy bottom with occasional boulders. As you approach the point itself, the bottom is rocky with a gradual slope. Off the point is a deep vertical drop-off. You can choose your own maximum depth. Visibility is 30 to 40 feet. Bull kelp is fairly thick along the bank and in the shallows.

Dive Profile

We entered the water 200 yards east from the tip of the point and drifted toward the point on the tail end of a rising tide.

Because of the variety of habitat, lots of different kinds of creatures can be seen here. White and orange anemones, purple sea urchins, rock scallops, cup coral, and sponge encrust the rocks. Kelp crab and greenling are not uncommon. Lemon peel nudibranchs, several kinds of sea stars, including large sunflower stars, and red sea cucumbers inhabit the sandy areas. Closer to the point, we saw cabezon, many kinds of rockfish, and big lingcod.

Directions

Alden Point is located on the NW tip of Patos Island. Alden Point is 4.34 miles (39 degrees) from Skipjack and 2.21 miles (50 degrees) from Boundary Pass Marker Buoy. You can launch your boat at Deception Pass, Flounder Bay, Washington Park, Cap Sante in Anacortes, or Bellingham. If you are driving to the islands, you can launch at Roche Harbor Boatel, Snug Harbor Marina, or San Juan County Park, all on San Juan Island; or at Rosario, Deer Harbor, Terrill Beach or West Beach on Orcas Island.

Patos Island, excluding the lighthouse reservation, is a Marine State Park with campsites, mooring buoys, and firepits. However, the number of facilities is very small, and there is no fresh water. The island was named by Spanish explorers who probably called it after ducks they saw there.

Hazards

There is heavy current on all exchanges so dive only when there is a minimal exchange. Be aware that there is a lot of fishing at times on and around the point itself. Use caution when thick fogs cover the area during the spring and fall. Winds can make Boundary Pass quite rough in the afternoon. Echo Bay on Sucia Island is protected from west weather and good anchorage can be had in 4 - 5 fathoms of water near the head.

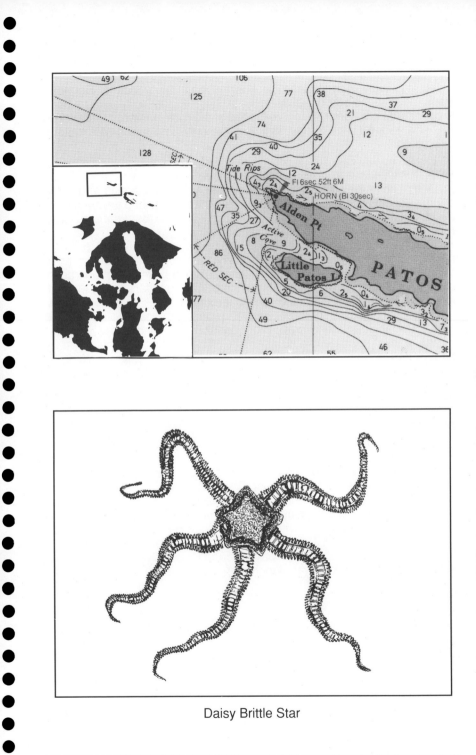

Daisy Brittle Star

㊲ BOUNDARY PASS MARKER BOUY

Habitat and Depth

This buoy marks a large rock formation in the middle of Boundary Pass, close to the border between the U.S. and Canada. Maximum depth is unlimited. It is about 35 feet to the top of the rock. Visibility ranges from 30 to 50 feet on a calm day, which is the only time this dive should be attempted.

Dive Profile

We dove the slack on a calm day with minimal tidal exchange. Our depth varied down to 100 feet as we circled the rock. (Keep an eye on your depth gauge as you descend. If you reach 100 ft. without contacting the rock, you need to return to the surface and try again.)

As you follow the wall down, you are immediately struck by the numbers of anemones. If you look carefully, there are white, green, orange, and pink tipped varieties to enjoy. There are several shades of encrusting sponge and some cup coral. There were purple sea stars and gray brittle stars. All in all, it is a very colorful background.

Lots of pecten scalops live here and some rock scallops, as well. We saw a Puget Sound king crab, probably about 10 inches across and a hermit crab. There were a number of exotic-looking basket stars at the deeper levels.

Swimming freely were several types of rockfish. We saw a black and yellow rockfish, several quillbacks and many brown ones. The lingcod here were really large.

Directions

Boundary Pass Marker Buoy is located 4.13 miles (323 degrees) from Pt. Doughty on Orcas Island and 2.3 miles (26 degrees) from the marker at Skipjack Island. You can launch your boat at Deception Pass, Flounder Bay, Washington Park, or Cap Sante in Anacortes. If you are ferrying your boat to the islands, you can launch at Roche Harbor Boatel, Snug Harbor Marina, or San Juan County Park, all on San Juan Island; or at Rosario, Deer Harbor, Terrill Beach, or West Beach on Orcas Island.

The International Boundary between Canada and the U.S. runs through Boundary Pass. Small bays around Patos Island are the closest place to anchor for a pleasant lunch stop. (See Alden Point dive.)

Hazards

The flood current sets north and the ebb current sets south. Ebb will generally produce a greater current velocity than the flood. The flood sets east on both sides of Sucia Island and Alden Banks.

Heavy fog is often a consideration during the spring and fall. The current can be dangerous. Do watch your depth; you can get deep very quickly. Keep an eye on the weather. You are in the middle of the strait with no protection. Winds can make Boundary Pass quite rough in the afternoon. (See Alden Point dive for shelter information.)

This must always be a live boat dive as you are a long, long swim from any shore. Only attempt this dive on a calm day with favorable tides.

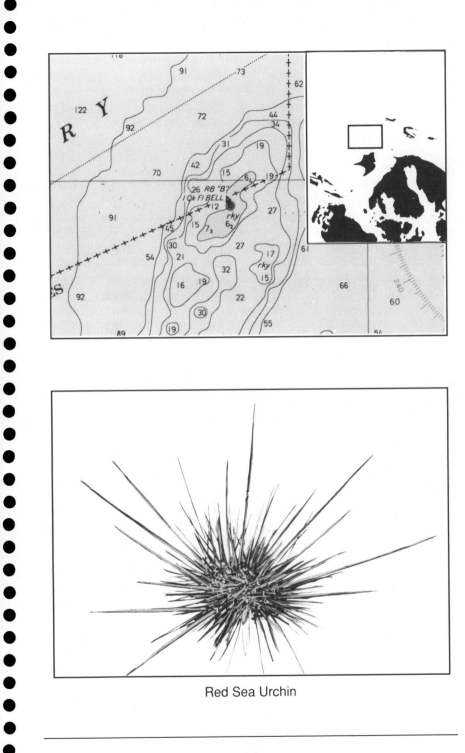

Red Sea Urchin

Habitat and Depth

Do not confuse this dive with Eagle Point on San Juan Island. This Eagle Point is located on the rocky western shore of Matia Island, north of Orcas Island. It is very deep here so you can choose your maximum depth. Visibility ranges from 20 to 30 feet. Kelp is growing on the point and along the wall. It does not present a problem.

Dive Profile

We entered the water just off the point on a high slack tide and drifted 200 feet to the southeast.

The area around the point itself consists of typical vertical walls covered with several types of anemones, especially the large plumed white ones. The most vertical area is on the point itself. As you move to the southeast, the drop-off becomes less steep. Rock walls give way to great boulders and sand with occasional outcroppings of rock which are covered with bryozoa, red and purple sea urchins, and sponge. Pecten scallops are abundant. We have found octopuses here and quillback rockfish. There are box crab as well as large lingcod. Lemon peel and striped nudibranchs live in the sand.

Directions

Eagle Pount is on the NW point of Matia Island. It is 2.3 miles (54 degrees) from Parker Reef Buoy (off Orcas) and 1.56 miles (94 degrees) from Johnson Point on Sucia Island. You can launch your boat at Deception Pass, Flounder Bay, Washington Park, Cap Sante in Anacortes, or Bellingham. If you are driving to the Islands, you can launch at Roche Harbor Boatel, Snug Harbor Marina, or San Juan County Park, all on San Juan Island; or at Rosario, Deer Harbor, Terrill Beach, or West Beach on Orcas Island.

Matia Island has campsites along its western coves. There are firepits, tables, water and toilets here. However, there is only moorage for six boats and the area is open to winter storms. Wildlife is protected here and you will see many varieties, including bald eagles.

The name of the island is usually pronounced "May-sha" (not what the Spanish explorer Franciso Eliza, who named it, intended), but you may hear a variety of other pronunciations as well.

Hazards

Current and heavy sport fishing must always be expected around the point. There is often thick fog during the spring and fall. Winds can make Boundary Pass quite rough in the afternoon. (See Alden Point dive for shelter information.)

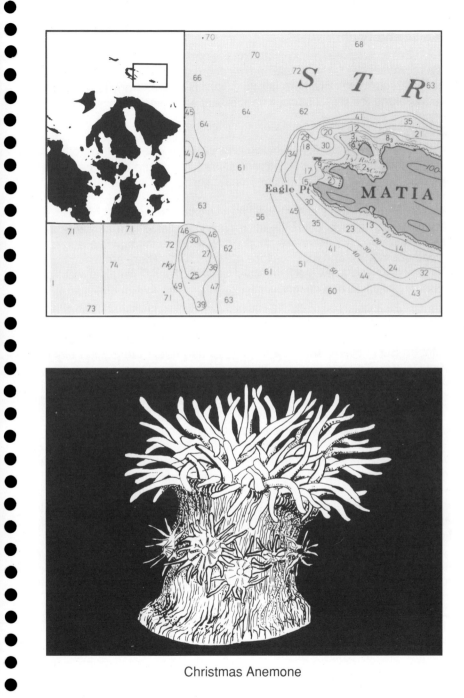

Christmas Anemone

Habitat and Depth

Ewing is a small, rocky island off the northeast coast of Sucia Island. The rock walls are fairly vertical and the entire descent is rather steep. You can pick your own maximum depth. Visibility ranges from 15 to 30 feet. Kelp is along the wall, but does not present a problem.

Dive Profile

We entered the water on the northwest tip of Ewing Island, just in front of the shallow channel to Ewing Cove. We drifted along the wall on a falling tide and rounded the southeast corner out of the current for a pickup.

Where the walls are vertical, they are packed with life. The rocks themselves host cup coral, deadman's fingers, staghorn bryozoa, and encrusting sponge. Red sea gherkins, colorful urchins, white and pink tipped anemones, and rock scallops are here also. There are a number of red rock crab and a few medium-sized lingcod. There are lots of rock fish: copper, quillback, and canary.

Directions

Ewing Island is located 0.73 of a mile (360 degrees) from Johnson Point on Sucia Island and 1.52 miles (310 degrees) from Eagle Point on Matia Island. You can launch your boat at Deception Pass, Flounder Bay, Washington Park, Cap Sante in Anacortes, or Bellingham. If you are driving to the islands, you can launch at Roche Harbor Boatel, Snug Harbor Marina, or San Juan County Park, all on San Juan Island; or at Rosario, Deer Harbor, Terrill Beach or West Beach on Orcas Island.

Ewing Island itself does not have much in the way of amenities. But Sucia Island State Park is one of the most popular marine recreation areas in the San Juans. Fossil Bay has two docks and Echo Bay has sixteen mooring buoys. There are another thirty or so scattered around Sucia's many bays. However, because of the enormous volume of boat traffic, they are often all in use during the summer months. Sucia has campsites, firepits, restrooms, toilet tank disposal, and water.

Much of its appeal comes from its varied scenery. There are evergreen forests, rock or sand or gravel beaches, and fantastically eroded rocks at Fox Cove. Sucia is well worth exploring, but don't be surprised if the facilities are full.

Hazards

Be alert for heavy pleasure boat traffic. Expect thick fog during the spring and fall. Winds can make Boundary Pass quite rough in the afternoon. (See Alden Point dive for shelter information.)

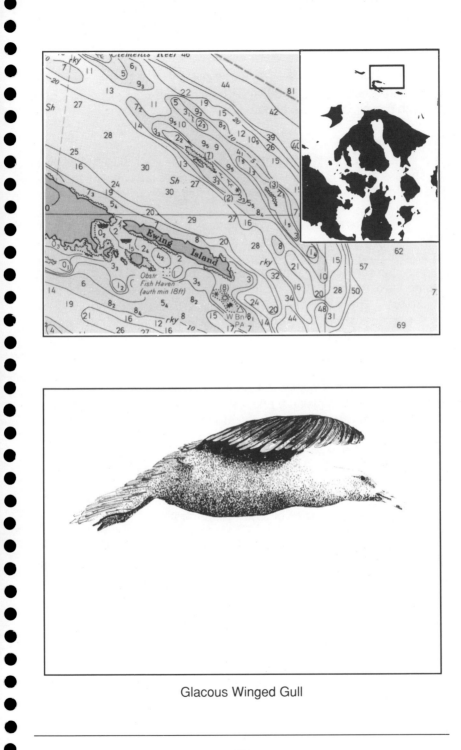

Glacous Winged Gull

(40) FLATTOP ISLAND

Habitat and Depth

Flattop Island offers excellent wall diving with wide shelves. Depth is unlimited. Visibility is 20 to 30 feet. There are kelp beds. Choose a calm day with a minimal tidal exchange.

Dive Profile

We dove on a slack tide and entered on the north side and followed the shelves around to the west. The first shelf goes out about 40 to 50 feet and then drops off to 100 feet. The second shelf goes out for some distance and than drops again.

This is a terrific dive for a photographer because of all the different types of creatures you encounter. Urchins are there in all sizes and colors, as are nudibranchs and both types of scallops. Barnacles, ribbed keyhole limpets, cup coral, and giant chiton encrust the rocks. You will find lots of anemones of various colors. Both wolfeels and octopuses were hiding in the crevices. There are basket stars and Puget Sound king crab. Here you will see schools of rockfish: browns, quillback, and copper. There are also cabezon and lingcod.

Directions

Flattop Island is located 2.43 miles (10 degrees) from O'Neil Island, Rocky Bay, San Juan Island, and 1.91 miles (322 degrees) from Jones Island. You can launch your boat at Deception Pass, Flounder Bay, Washington Park, or Cap Sante in Anacortes. If you are ferrying your boat to the islands, you can launch at Roche Harbor Boatel, Snug Harbor Marina, or San Juan County Park, all on San Juan Island; or Rosario, Deer Harbor, Terrill Beach, or West Beach on Orcas Island.

Prevost Harbor and Reid Harbor-offer moorage and access to the picnic and camping facilities of Stuart Island State Park. (See Turn Point dive for facilities information.)

Flattop Island's name is descriptive of its appearance. It is part of the San Juan Island Wilderness. Formerly, small boats were allowed to land on the beach. However, this is now prohibited so that seabirds can nest here undisturbed. Therefore, Flattop Island must be a live boat dive.

Hazards

Don't be surprised at the thickness of the fog during the spring and fall. Winds can make President Channel and San Juan Channel quite rough in the afternoon. Deer Harbor, Roche Harbor, West Sound, and Friday Harbor are all within easy reach.

Kelp Crab

Habitat and Depth

Johnson Point is located on the southeast side of Sucia Island, north of Fossil Bay. It is a rocky area with sand between the large boulders. Visibility is 20 to 30 feet. You can choose your own maximum depth. Kelp is present.

Dive Profile

We dove just before the start of a falling tide. Our entry was at the northwest corner of the point shown on NOAA chart 18421.

The rocks here are covered with white anemones, cup coral, and encrusting sponge. We found pecten scallops, kelp crab, red rock crab, red sea urchins, and basket stars. There are large octopuses and wolf eels. The area supports greenling, many perch, and small lingcod. As the tide began to ebb, the visibility continued to diminish down to almost zero on the point itself. We were able to get behind some large boulders for a rest stop.

Directions

Johnson Point is located 3.43 miles (50 degrees) from Pt. Doughty and 1.43 miles (16 degrees) from the Parker Reef light. You can launch your boat at Deception Pass, Flounder Bay, Washington Park, Cap Sante in Anacortes, or Bellingham. If you are driving to the islands, you can launch at Rosario, Deer Harbor, Terrill Beach or West Beach, all on Orcas Island.

Sucia Island is a Marine State Park. It has over fifty campsites with firepits, drinking water, restrooms, toilet tank disposal, and also moorage for over seventy boats. However, because of its unique beauty, it is heavily used. Often in the summer months all of its facilities are full. (See Ewing Island dive for further information.)

Hazards

Spring and fall fogs can be very thick. Winds can make Boundary Pass and the Strait of Georgia quite rough in the afternoon. (See Alden Point dive for shelter information.)

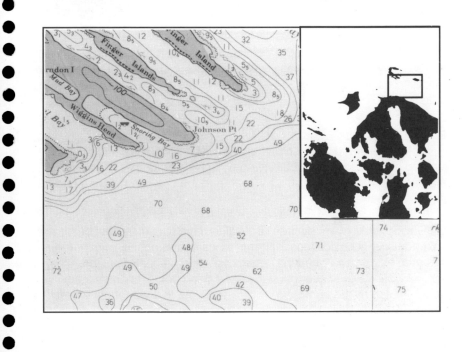

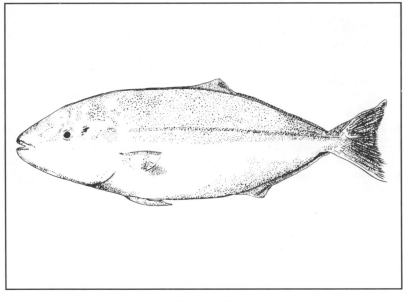

Yellowtail

Habitat and Depth

Our preferred dive is the rocky reef located in the north bay, although you can dive the bluffs along with everyone else. Depth is unlimited. Visibility ranges from 20 to 35 feet. There is lots of kelp during the growing season.

Dive Profile

Most divers dive the bluffs and crowd the bay. We find the reef, located about 100 yards out in the bay, to be a better bet. The reef is marked and easily accessible by boat, and the bay has mooring buoys. We dove on the slack.

There are lots of fish here: greenlings, cabezon, small lingcod, quillbacks, and brown, copper, and china rockfish. The rocks of the reef host abalone, rock scallops, different kinds of anemones, purple and red sea urchins, red sea gherkins, lemon peel and alabaster nudibranchs.

If you like to scavenge, there are fishing poles, anchors, dive gear, etc. left by the summer crowds. It is best to dive here in winter when you will usually have the whole bay to yourself.

Directions

Jones Island is located 0.65 of a mile (277 degrees) from Steep Point, the western tip of Orcas Island, and 1.73 miles (70 degrees) from O'Neil Island. You can launch your boat at Deception Pass, Flounder Bay, Washington Park, or Cap Sante in Anacortes. If you are ferrying your boat to the islands, you can launch at Roche Harbor Boatel, Snug Harbor Marina, or San Juan County Park, all on San Juan Island; or at Rosario, Deer Harbor, Terrill Beach, or West Beach on Orcas Island.

Jones Island is named for Jacob Jones, a U.S. captain in the War of 1812. Jones Island State Park is quite popular in the summer. The north bay has a float, mooring buoys, campsites, and picnic tables. If the buoys are full, be advised that it is difficult to secure an anchor on the rocky bottom. There are hiking trails, drinking water, and restrooms. You will probably see a variety of wildlife here.

Hazards

This area has thick fog during the spring and fall. Winds can make President Channel and San Juan Channel quite rough in the afternoon. (See Flattop Island dive for shelter information.)

The biggest hazard is the current which can move right over the reef and sweep you around to the other side of the island. You must use a live boat to be safe. Boat traffic is very heavy in the summer.

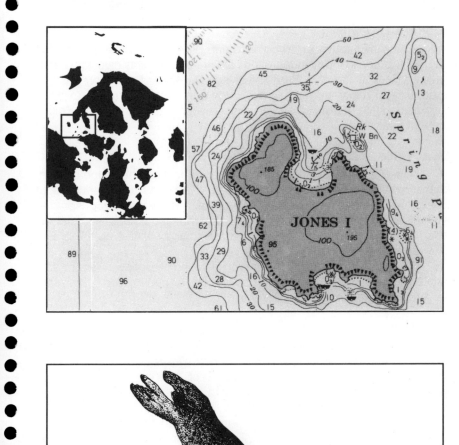

Harbor Seal

(43) LAWSON BLUFF

Habitat and Depth

Lawson Bluff forms the northwestern curve of Sucia Island, just to the north of the Shallow Bay indentation. Do not confuse this dive with either Lawson Rock in Thatcher Pass or Lawson Reef near Deception Pass. It is an area of rocky ledges, big boulders, and passageways to explore. Visibility is 20 to 40 feet. You can choose your maximum depth. Kelp is present near shore.

Dive Profile

We dove on a flood tide, entering the water about the midpoint of the bluff and drifting south toward Shallow Bay. It is a good idea to bring a light to explore the passageways and little caves. There are octopuses and wolfeels living in them. Rock scallops, abalone, and colorful sea urchins also make their homes on these rocks. Nudibranchs live on the gravel covered ledges.

It is a good place to see lots of rockfish and greenling. We also saw basket stars and Puget Sound king crab. This is a popular sport fishing spot so you will often find lost fishing gear.

Directions

Lawson Bluff is located on the NNW section of Sucia Island. It is located 3.78 miles (89 degrees) from Boundary Pass Buoy and 1.34 miles (244 degrees) from the buoy at Clements Reef. You can launch your boat at Deception Pass, Flounder Bay, Washington Park, Cap Sante in Anacortes, or Bellingham. If you are driving to the islands, you can launch at Roche Harbor Boatel, Snug Harbor Marina, or San Juan County park, all on San Juan Island; or at Rosario, Deer Harbor, Terrill Beach, or West Beach on Orcas Island.

Sucia Island State Park appeals to just about everyone. The lovely scenery ranges from evergreen forest to beaches with bizarre rock formations. There are six miles of hiking trails, campsites, firepits, and water available. Sucia also has restrooms and toilet tank disposal. Fossil Bay has two docks and there are more than forty mooring buoys spread over various small bays. Unfortunateiy, all of these facilities are not enough to accomodate the large volume of visitors who are drawn to Sucia each summer. Don't be surprised if every moorage is taken.

Hazards

Always consider the possibility of heavy fog during the spring and fall. Winds can make the Strait of Georgia quite rough in the afternoon. (See Alden Point dive for shelter information.) This is a popular fishing area and heavy pleasure boat traffic can pose a hazard.

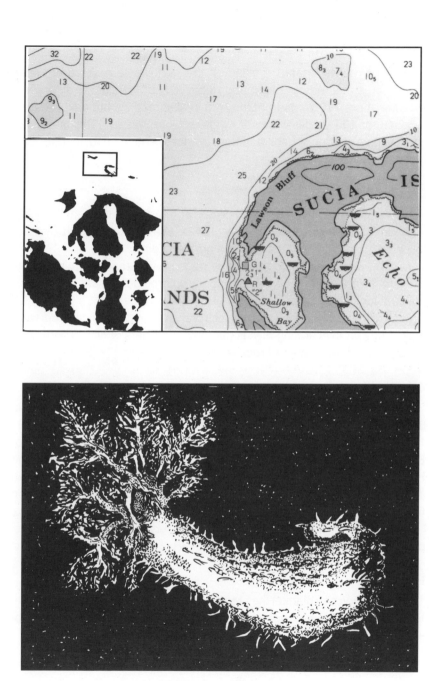

White Sea Gherkin

(44) **PARKER REEF**

Habitat and Depth

This reef is located 7 miles off the northwestern shore of Orcas Island. It is marked by a light and uncovered at low tide. Parker Reef extends about 110 yards from the light in all directions but east, where it reaches for 160 yards. Visibility range is 15 to 30 feet. This is a good, shallow dive in a rocky habitat. There is a lot to see at 30 to 40 feet. Kelp is present.

Dive Profile

We dove just before a flood tide and entered the water near the reef's southern tip as shown on NOAA chart 18421. We descended to 40 feet and followed the contours of the reef in a northerly direction.

The usual white and green anemones and red and purple urchins clung to the boulders. There were brightly colored ochre seastars and the unusual-looking daisy brittle star.

We found octopuses and red rock crab among the boulders, but what makes this an exhilarating dive is the sheer numbers of fish. There were schools of different types of rockfish and some lingcod as well.

Directions

Parker Reef is located 2.43 miles (70 degrees) from Pt. Doughty and 3.17 miles (249 degrees) from Puffin Island. You can launch at Deception Pass, Flounder Bay, Washington Park, Cap Sante in Anacortes, or Bellingham. If you are driving to the islands, you can launch at Roche Harbor Boatel, Snug Harbor Marina, or San Juan County Park, all on San Juan Island; or at Rosario, Deer Harbor, Terrill Beach, or West Beach on Orcas Island.

Nearby Pt. Doughty Recreation Site has a couple of campsites, picnic facilities, and restrooms.

Hazards

Thick fog can blanket the area in the spring and fall. Winds can make Boundary Pass quite rough in the afternoon. (See Alden Point dive for shelter information.)

Tiger Rockfish

Habitat and Depth

Point Disney is a spectacular 600 foot cliff at the southwestern tip of Waldron Island. The cliff continues steeply underwater and you can select a depth from 40 feet to much deeper. Visibility ranges from 20 to 30 feet. There is kelp along the shore.

Dive Profile

Since the southern exposure of Waldron Island is in a high current area on both the ebb and flood tides, we chose to dive on a slack ebb. Slack water is usually not long enough to complete your dive, so part can be made on a slow drift. Entering the water on the south side of the point itself, we slowly moved in a northeasterly direction and finished on a rising tide.

This is a very beautiful dive, notable for the white and green anemones sharing space with colonies of barnacles, yellow boring sponge, red sea urchins, and ivory toned basket stars. There are rock and pecten scallops here as well as a number of octopus dens. You will also find numerous rockfish, kelp greenling, and lingcod.

Directions

Point Disney is located on the SSW tip of Waldron Island, 3.26 miles (004 degrees) north of Jones Island and 2.13 miles (41 degrees) from Flattop Island. You can launch your boat at Deception Pass, Flounder Bay, Washington Park, or Cap Sante in Anacortes. If you are driving to the islands, you can launch at Roche Harbor Boatel, Snug Harbor Marina, or San Juan County Park, all on San Juan Island; or at Rosario, Deer Harbor, Terrill Beach, or West Beach on Orcas Island.

Point Disney was named for a member of the Wilkes Expedition which explored much of the area. There are a number of sand and gravel beaches scattered around Waldron Island, but only the tidelands are public. Anchorage in Cowlitz and Mail Bays is not the best, even in mild weather. The island is noted for the numbers of bald eagles who regularly nest here.

Hazards

During the spring and fall, fog can be heavy. Winds can make President Channel quite rough in the afternoon. (See Alden Point dive for shelter information.)

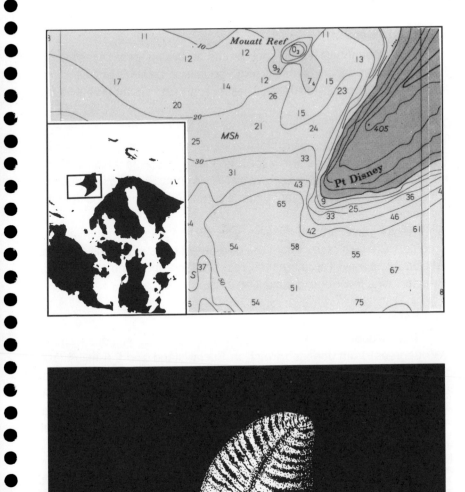

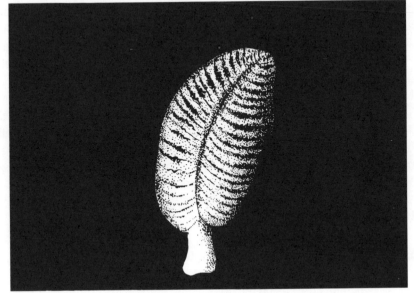

Sea Penn

Habitat and Depth

Point Doughty is a bare knob on the northwest tip of Orcas Island. The underwater habitat is mainly large boulders. Depth is unlimited and visibility ranges from 25 to 40 feet. There is kelp present almost year round.

Dive Profile

This is a fairly easy dive, close to shore, and a short run from nearby resorts. We dove on a slack low tide and entered the water at the rocks on the south side of the point, as shown on NOAA chart 18421. We drifted out to the point. As the tide began to run, it carried us around the point to the north side.

As you pass through the kelp, you will notice lots of greenling and some northern kelp crab. There are colonies of red sea urchins attached to the boulders as well as anemones, rock scallops, and some basket stars. We also saw a few Puget Sound king crab.

Directions

Point Doughty is located on the NW point of Orcas Island, 3.47 miles (230 degrees) from Johnson Point on Sucia Island and 2.5 miles (105 degrees) from Pt. Hammond on Waldron Island. You can launch your boat at Deception Pass, Flounder Bay, Washington Park, or Cap Sante in Anacortes. If you are ferrying your boat to the islands, you can launch at Roche Harbor Boatel, Snug Harbor Marina, or San Juan County Park, all on San Juan Islands or at Rosario, Deer Harbor, Terrill Beach, or West Beach on Orcas Island.

Point Doughty is named for a member of the Wilkes Expedition. There is limited camping area available, but it is only accessible to small boats that can be beached. Anchorage is really poor and submerged rocks make landing an adventure. The only trail into the area is limited to use by YMCA campers. Eagles nest around here.

Hazards

Thick fog is often present in the spring and fall. Winds can make President Channel quite rough in the afternoon. (See Alden Point dive for shelter information.)

Watch for currents on the point itself. Turning the corner will get you out of the main current. Boat traffic is especially heavy in the summer.

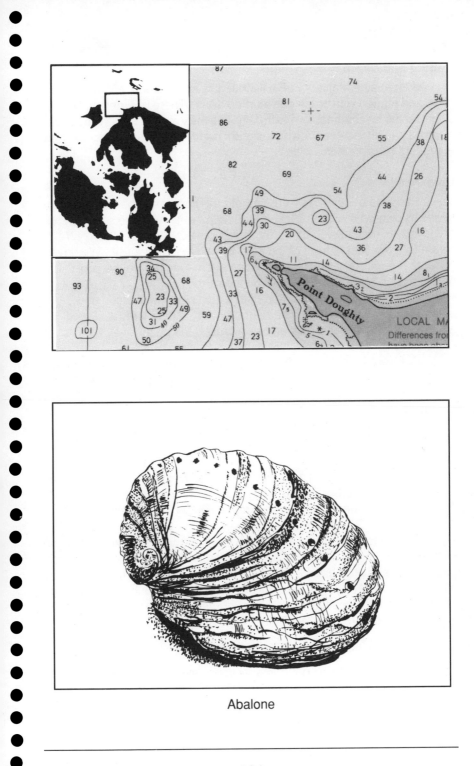

Abalone

Habitat and Depth

Just east of Matia is Puffin Island. It is steep-sided, about forty feet high, and topped with brush and stunted trees. There is a reef, marked by a light, at the far southeastern extremity. Visibility ranges from 10 to 20 feet, and you can choose your own maximum depth in this rocky habitat. Kelp is present all around the island.

Dive Profile

Because of strong current on both the flood and ebb tides, we chose to dive on the high slack. Our point of entry was the southern tip of ths island, just outside the buoy shown on NOAA chart 18421. We swam to a few feet in front of the kelp and dove just below it. We dove down to a depth of 40 - 60 feet. It didn't seem long before the tide began to ebb and we were swept off the reef.

One of the striking features of this dive was the masses and masses of large white plumed sea anemones. There were rock and pecten scallops and red rock and kelp crab. Octopuses live in the small rocky caves.

We were joined by harbor seals who were either curious about us or were hunting the abundant rockfish and the big lingcod that we saw.

Directions

Puffin Island is located 3.04 miles (315 degrees) from Clark Island and 4.21 miles (267 degrees) from Pt. Migley on Lummi Island. You can launch your boat at Deception Pass, Flounder Bay, Washington Park, Cap Sante in Anacortes, or Bellingham. If you are driving to the islands, you can launch at Roche Harbor Boatel, Snug Harbor Marina, or San Juan County Park, all on San Juan Island; or at Rosario, Deer Harbor, Terrill Beach, or West Beach on Orcas Island.

Puffin Island is named after those rather peculiar seabirds that seem to fly underwater. It is part of the San Juan Island Wilderness Area and going ashore is prohibited. There are colonies of puffins (naturally) and other seabirds; keep your boat clear so as not to disturb them. Matia Island State Park has campsites, firepits, restrooms, and moorage and makes a good lunch stop. (See Eagle Point, Matia Island dive.)

Hazards

Plan for the heavy spring and fall fogs. Winds can make Boundary Pass quite rough in the afternoon. (See Alden Point dive for shelter information.) The current here is very strong, so dive on the slack.

Tufted Puffin

Habitat and Depth

Raccoon Point, on Orcas Island's northeast shore, is just opposite Matia Island. It has vertical walls, big boulders, sand and gravel ledges, and unlimited depth. Take a light with you and be sure to dive when the sun is high. The shadows from the bluffs above can make this as dark as a night dive.

Dive Profile

We dove on a falling tide, entering the water on the point shown on NOAA chart 18421 and drifting to the southeast.

There are lots of things to see on this dive, plus it is a good opportunity to practice night diving techniques in the daytime! We found wolfeels in small crevices, basket stars, red rock crab and striped nudibranchs. There are pecten scallops, greenling, lots of copper and quillback rockfish, and a few small lingcod. Anemones and urchins cover the rocks.

This is a good dive for observing, but not a good dive for hunting fish because of the insufficient light.

Directions

Raccoon Point is located on the northeast side of Orcas Island. It is 2.78 miles (192 degrees) from Puffin Island and 2.43 miles (261 degrees) from the northern point of Barnes Island. You can launch your boat at Deception Pass, Flounder Bay, Washington Park, Cap Sante in Anacortes, or Bellingham. If you are driving to the islands, you can launch at Roche Harbor Boatel, Snug Harbor Marina, or San Juan County Park, all on San Juan Island; or at Rosario, Deer Harbor, Terrill Beach, or West Beach on Orcas Island.

There are no amenities at Raccoon Point. Please note that only the tidelands are public on this part of Orcas. A better bet for a pleasant stop is either Matia or Clark Island. Both have campsites, restrooms, firepits, and moorage. (See Eagle Point, Matia Island dive.)

Hazards

Be aware that thick fogs often cover the area in the spring and fall. Winds can make Boundary Pass quite rough in the afternoon. (See Alden Point dive for shelter information.) Don't forget to bring your light.

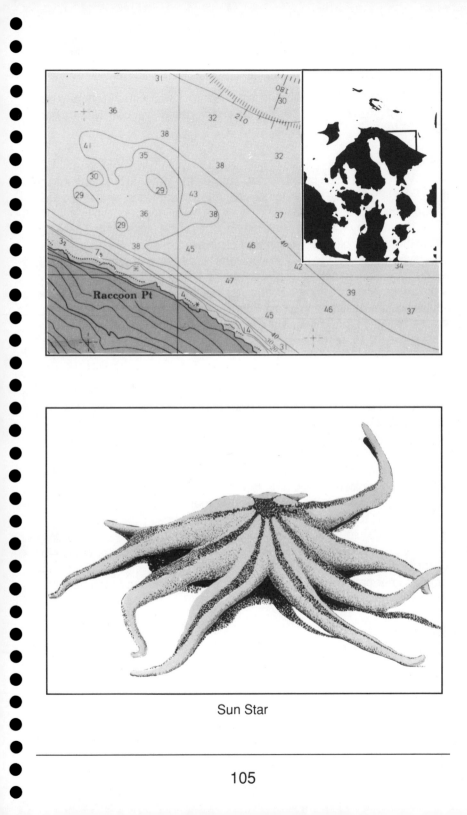

Sun Star

(49) SKIPJACK ISLAND

Habitat and Depth

The north side of this island is a sheer rock wall with a large kelp bed in front of it. You can choose your maximum depth. Visibility ranges from 20 to 40 feet.

Dive Profile

We dove a slack high tide and entered the water at the north end of the island. As the tide began to fall, we drifted towards the west and exited beyond the kelp.

If you enjoy watching seals playing, this is the place for it. There are lots of them here, gliding through the kelp down to a depth of about 40 feet. When you get below the kelp, the gradual slope of the wall steepens. You will find pecten and rock scallops and abalone. The wall is colorfully painted with various kinds of anemones and urchins, white encrusting sponge, and several colors of algae. We saw Puget Sound king crab, basket stars, all kinds of rockfish, greenling, a red Irish lord, and lingcod. Photographers have plenty of subjects here.

Directions

Skipjack Island is located 3.52 miles (296 degrees) from Pt. Doughty and 2.08 miles (201 degrees) from Boundary Pass Marker Buoy. You can launch your boat at Deception Pass, Flounder Bay, Washington Park, or Cap Sante in Anacortes. If you are ferrying your boat to the islands, you can launch at Roche Harbor Boatel, Snug Harbor Marina, or San Juan County Park, all on San Juan Island; or at Rosario, Deer Harbor, Terrill Beach, or West Beach on Orcas Island.

Skipjack Island is a wildlife refuge that is closed to the public. It contains large rockeries of various kinds of seabirds. Stay as far from the island as possible to avoid frightening them from their nests. Waldron Island is close but doesn't offer very good anchorage. A better choice for a rest stop is either Stuart or Sucia Island. (See Ewing Island dive for facilities information.) Skipjack Island is probably named for the fish that were commonly found here.

Hazards

You can expect thick spring and fall fogs. Winds can make Boundary Pass quite rough in the afternoon. Avoid running too close to the rocks and kelp. (See Alden Point dive for shelter information.) Current is the only real hazard, but be alert for sport fishermen jigging for cod.

Pelagic Cormorant

Habitat and Depth

Toe Point is located on the eastern side of Patos Island, the most northerly of the San Juans. The toe-shaped projection is about 60 feet high and formed of erosion resistant rock that remained after the softer substances around it had been worn away. Visibility is 20 to 30 feet and you can choose your own maximum depth. There are large boulders, rocky outcroppings, and some vertical wall. Kelp is present along the bank but does not pose a problem.

Dive Profile

We entered the water at the most southern point and 300 feet to the west as shown on NOAA chart 18421. Because we dove on a falling tide, we were out of the main flow, but this was an easy drift dive. The walls and rocks are thickly covered with invertebrate life forms. There are many urchins, anemones, bryozoa, rock scallops, red sea gherkins, and nudibranchs.

You will find octopuses here and lots and lots of fish. We saw all types of rockfish, cabezon, greenling, and big lingcod.

Directions

Toe Point is located 1.43 miles (324 degrees) from Lawson Bluff and 4.86 miles (49 degrees) from Skipjack Island. You can launch your boat at Deception Pass, Flounder Bay, Washington Park, Cap Sante in Anacortes, or Bellingham. If you are driving to the islands, you can launch at Roche Harbor Boatel, Snug Harbor Marina, or San Juan County Park, all on San Juan Island; or at Rosario, Deer Harbor, Terrill Beach, or West Beach on Orcas Island.

All of Patos Island excepting the lighthouse reservation at Alden Point is a Marine State Park, but there are only four actual campsites and two mooring buoys. There are firepits and restrooms, but no fresh water.

Hazards

There is a strong possibility of heavy fog during the spring and fall. Winds can make Boundary Pass quite rough in the afternoon. (See Alden Point dive for shelter information.)

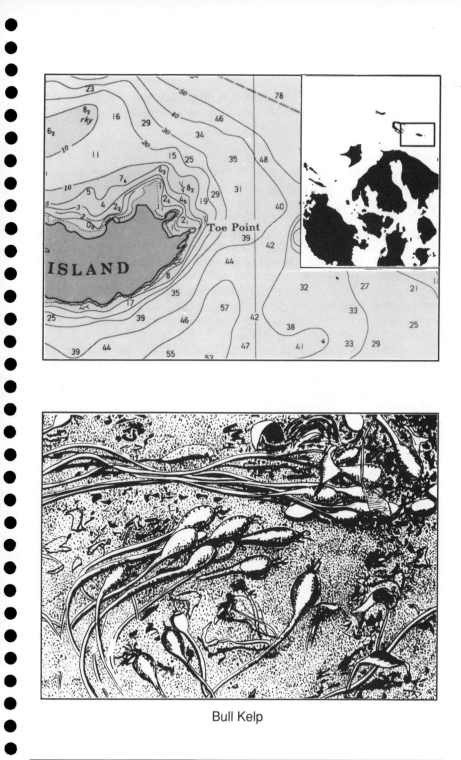

Bull Kelp

WHITE ROCK

Habitat and Depth

White Rock is part of a shallow reef. Maximum depth is unlimited on the north end. It is 15 feet to the top of the reef. Visibility ranges from 30 to 50 feet. Kelp is present.

Dive Profile

We entered the water on the north side of the rock on a high slack. We descended to 30 feet and moved in a NNW direction parallel to the reef while increasing our depth.

If you enjoy seeing sea mammals, this is the place to spot seals. They hunt the large kelp bed which is due east of the reef. Greenling and small fish hide in the kelp. Often the seals will dive right along with you.

The reef rocks are covered with white and green anemones. You will find pecten scallops and rock scallops, and abalone live on the rocks. We saw a china rockfish by its home crevice, brown rockfish, cabezon, painted greenling and lingcod. We notice that we seem to see many more fish during the spring and early summer months than later. Perhaps this is because of increased fishing pressure during the summer season or because the fish tend to move much deeper when the summer sun penetrates the water.

You will find old practice bombs dating from the late 1960s. The bombs were loaded with 12 guage flares which would be visible at night.

Directions

White Rock is located l.l8 miles (245 degrees) from Pt. Disney, Waldron Island and 1.17 miles (017 degrees) from Flattop Island. You can launch your boat at Deception Pass, Flounder Bay, Washington Park, or Cap Sante in Anacortes. If you are ferrying your boat to the islands, you can launch at Roche Harbor Boatel, Snug Harbor Marina, or San Juan County Park, all on San Juan Island; or at Rosario, Deer Harbor, Terrill Beach, or West Beach on Orcas Island.

White Rock is part of the San Juan Wilderness Area. Since it is a bird refuge nesting area, the public is asked to stay away so the birds won't be disturbed. Nearby Waldron Island does not offer particularly good anchorage. You are better off heading west to Stuart Island or northwest to Sucia Island in search of a pleasant lunch stop. (See Ewing Island dive for facilities information.)

Hazards

Surface visibility can be affected by heavy fog during the spring and fall. Winds can make President Channel quite rough in the afternoon. (See Flattop Island and Alden Point dives for shelter information.)

Watch for heavy boat traffic in the summer when many people jig for cod in this area.

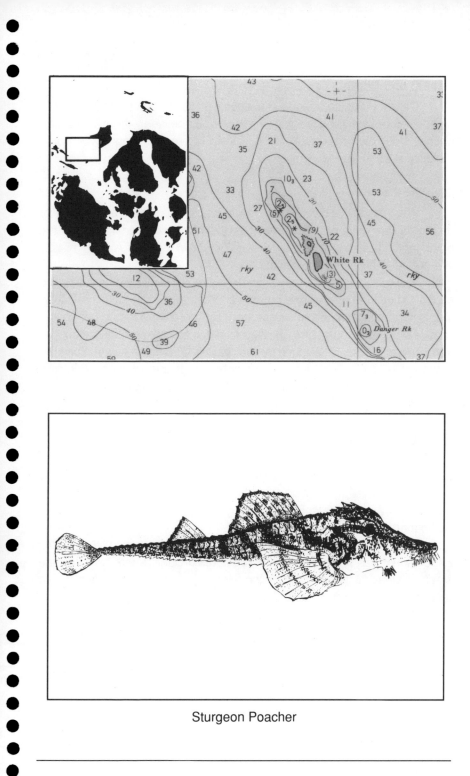

Sturgeon Poacher

(52) CARTER POINT

Habitat and Depth

Carter Point comprises the southern tip of Lummi Island. It is composed of rocky ledges with vertical walls between them. You can choose your own maximum depth. Kelp is present around the point. Visibility is 20 to 30 feet.

Dive Profile

What made this dive especially enjoyable was the excellent visibility on the day we dove it. We started our dive at the southeastern tip of the point, just in front of the shallow water line shown on NOAA chart 18421. We drifted NNW along the island.

The walls are very colorful, filled with just about everything you would expect to find in a rocky habitat: purple encrusting sponge, cup coral, dead man's fingers, green and white anemones. There were red sea gherkins, rock scallops, and sun stars. Pecten scallops are all over, as are copper and quillback rockfish. We saw two octopuses here as we swam along the ledges shining our lights into the many holes. It is always amazing how such a large invertebrate can manage to move through such a small opening.

Directions

Carter Point is located on the SSE tip of Lummi Island. It is 0.65 of a mile (51 degrees) from the NNW marker of Viti Rocks and 1.34 miles (261 degrees) from the marker on Eliza Rock. You can launch your boat at Deception Pass, Flounder Bay, Washington Park, Cap Sante in Anacortes, Bellingham, or Lummi Island.

Carter Point, named for William Carter, a member of the Wilkes Expedition of 1841, is approximately 30 acres of public shore. Above it are steep hillsides which are held by the federal government as a lighthouse reserve. Lummi Island Recreational Site, north and east of Carter Point, is a scenic area with swimming beaches and makes a nice lunch stop.

Hazards

This is an area of thick fog in the spring and fall. Winds can make Boundary Pass, Rosario Strait, and Bellingham Channel quite rough in the afternoon.

Arctic Loon

Habitat and Depth

Cone Islands are made up of five forested mini-islands and low tide rocks which lie off the northeast coast of Cypress Island. It is an interesting area of ledges, boulders, and vertical walls. You can choose your own maximum depth. Visibility ranges from 20 to 30 feet. Kelp is heavy.

Dive Profile

Our point of entry was the eastern tip of Cone Island (the largest and most easterly of the group), just in front of the shallow water line shown on NOAA chart 18421. We entered on a slight flood and were able to ride the current and circle the island.

This was a colorful dive. One area had bright yellow lemon peel nudibranchs; another had purple and green sea urchins and red sea gherkins. There were quite a few red rock crab, rock and pecten scallops, some kelp greenling, and copper and brown rockfish. We did not see any lingcod.

At about 40 to 60 feet on the north side, depending on the tide, you will encounter an abandoned fishing net. Several dead crab caught in it are a reminder of just how dangerous these hazards are to sea life.

Directions

Cone Island (the largest and most easterly one of the group) is 1.9 miles (126 degrees) from Towhead Island and 0.86 of a mile (274 degrees) from the shallow water mark off Clark Point on Guemes Island. You can launch your boat at Deception Pass, Flounder Bay, Washington Park, Cap Sante in Anacortes, or Bellingham.

Cone Islands are undeveloped state park land. The islands are steep sided bluffs with small rock and gravel beaches. There are 9.9 acres in all, but access is difficult and there are only two mooring buoys. Eagle Harbor or Deepwater Bay on Cypress Island are better choices for anchoring for a lunch stop.

Hazards

You may find heavy fog during the spring and fall. Winds can make Boundary Pass and Bellingham Channel quite rough on afternoons with a high exchange. It is best to travel back to Anacortes on the east side of Guemes Island for the most protection.

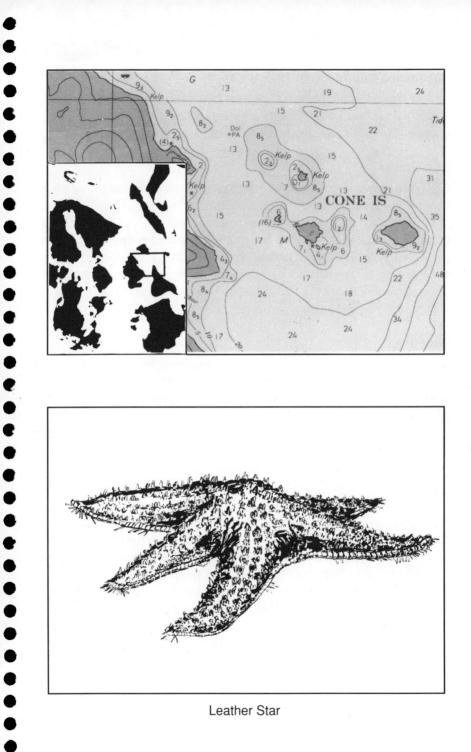

Leather Star

Habitat and Depth

This rocky patch north of Cypress Island is dangerous to boat traffic and is marked with a day beacon. It is exposed on low tides. You can choose your maximum depth. Visibility ranges fron 10 to 30 feet.

Dive Profile

We entered the water on the south side of the reef on a low slack tide. Our depth increased rapidly once we left the shallow reef itself.

Deep trenches 5 to 20 feet wide run across the reef and are fun to explore. Bring a light. You will find green, white plumed, pink tipped, and tiny zoanthid anemones. Rock scallops, abalone, and different colored sponge cling to the rock sides. There are many pecten scallops, basket stars, and some Puget Sound king crab. There are all kinds of rockfish, no big lingcod, but some large cabezon.

Directions

Cypress Reef is 0.26 of a mile (287 degrees) from Towhead Island and 0.78 of a mile (157 degrees) from Buckeye Shoal. You can launch your boat at Deception Pass, Flounder Bay, Washington Park, Cap Sante in Anacortes, or Bellingham.

Pelican Beach Recreation Site on the northeast side of Cypress Island makes a good lunch stop. There is clamming on the beach, camping, restrooms, and moorage. The views are scenic.

Hazards

Fog can present its own hazards in spring and fall. Winds can make Rosario Strait and the Strait of Georgia quite rough in the afternoon. The east sides of Cypress and Guemes Islands will provide you with enough wind protection to allow for a safe run back to Anacortes.

There is not much boat traffic here, just an occasional fisherman jigging for cod. However, the current can present a hazard. The area is a lot more open than it appears on the charts. It can get quite rough here with just a little wind out of any direction.

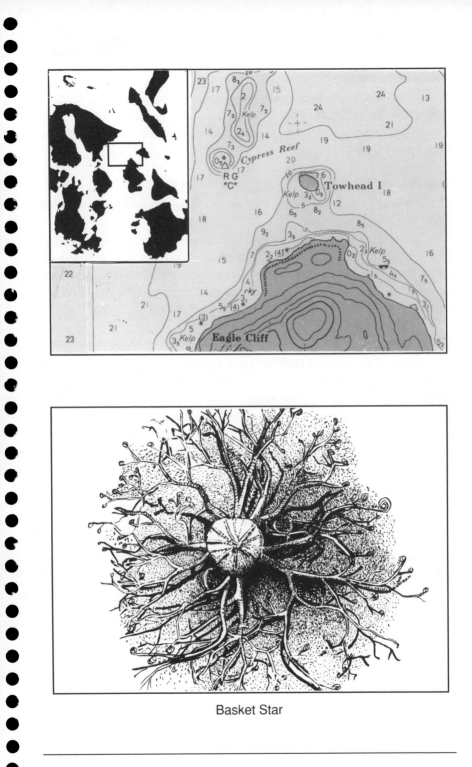

Basket Star

Habitat and Depth

Eagle Cliff is a high point along the northwest shore of Cypress Island. Maximum depth is about 70 feet. You can go deeper, but the habitat changes to gravel and mud and there is not much to see. Visibility ranges from 10 to 20 feet.

Dive Profile

This is an area very easy to dive. We entered right below the bluff, north of the long boulders.

This is not a very colorful dive, but there are big rock slides and lots of boulders with cracks and crevices in them. You need a light to explore them. There are lingcod here and many kinds of rockfish. You will probably see an octopus or two. Abalone, rock scallops, and small Puget Sound king crab can also be found here.

Directions

Eagle Cliff is on the NNW end of Cypress Island. It is 2.21 miles (85 degrees) from Lydia Shoal and 0.65 of a mile (186 degrees) from Cypress Reef. You can launch your boat at Deception Pass, Flounder Bay, Washington Park, Cap Sante in Anacortes, Bellingham, or Lummi Island.

There are some gravel beaches near the base of Eagle Cliff, but there is no trail up the cliff. Pelican Beach Recreational site on the northeast side of Cypress Island has a lovely view, camping and picnic facilities, restrooms, firepits, and moorage.

Hazards

Spring and fall can produce heavy fog. Winds can make Rosario Strait quite rough in the afternoon. Choose the east sides of Cypress and Guemes Islands for wind protection on your run back to Anacortes.

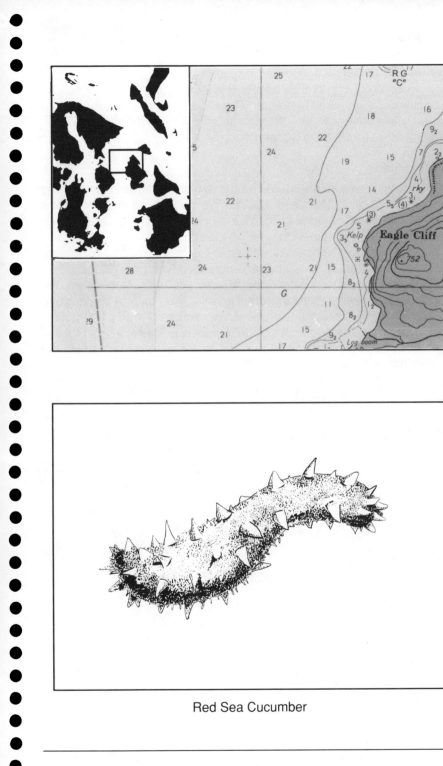

Red Sea Cucumber

⑤⑥ ELIZA ROCK

Habitat and Depth

Eliza (pronounced el EE za) Rock is located off the southern end of Eliza Island. It is marked by a light. There is a rocky pinnacle that slopes gradually into deeper water. You can choose your own maximum depth. Visibility ranges from 15 to 30 feet. Kelp is present.

Dive Profile

Our entry was on the southernmost tip of the rock, just in front of the marker shown on NOAA chart 18421. We descended and swam in a southerly direction to the point. Then we continued past the point and down the south slope of the pinnacle

Lots of rock fish of several varieties live here. We saw quillbacks, browns, and blacks. White plumed anemones, red and purple sea urchins, and rock scallops adhere to the slope. Pecten scallops are abundant. We found a large octopus, about eight feet across. We played a gentle game of tug with one of its tentacles for about five minutes. Finding an octopus, or as in this case a large octopus out in the open, is always special treat.

A number of harbor seals were snoozing on the rock but did not venture into the water while we were there. Later we tried our luck at fishing with buzz bombs but were only successful at catching and releasing four dog fish before tiring of our luck.

Directions

Eliza Rock is 1.86 miles (62 degrees) from the southern mark of Viti Rocks and 4.91 miles (51 degrees) from the east Cons Island. You can launch your boat at Deception Pass, Flounder Bay, Washington Park, Cap Sante in Anacortes, Bellingham, or Lummi Island.

Eliza Rock and Island were named for Francisco Eliza, a Spanish explorer who sailed the area in 1791. Lummi Island Recreation Site on the southeast side of Lummi Island is a pretty spot for a lunch stop and does have swimming beaches.

Hazards

Expect heavy fog during the spring and fall. Winds can make Boundary Pass and Bellingham Channel quite rough in the afternoon. It is a short run to Bellingham but the bay is windy also. You can gain protection from a south and west wind on the east side of Lummi Island.

Beware of dragging anchor here in heavy weather. The bottom around Eliza Island has poor holding ability. Be careful of the shallow water hazards especially on a low tide.

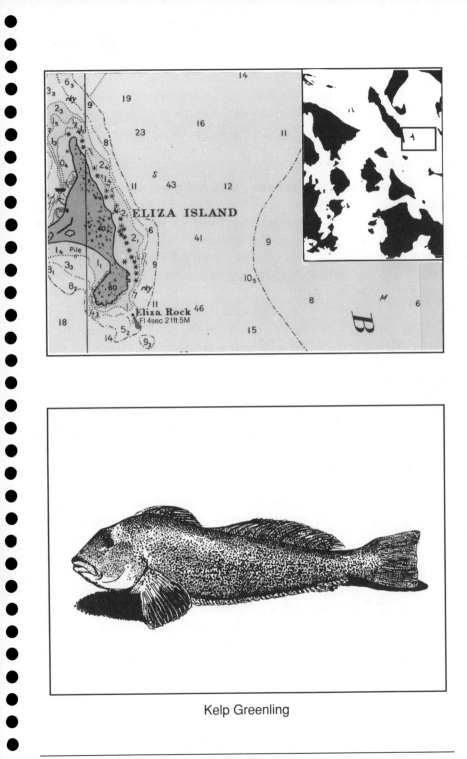

Kelp Greenling

(57) HAT/SADDLEBAG ISLANDS

Habitat and Depth

These islands sit on an underwater shelf near the entrance to Padilla Bay. The habitat is mud and eelgrass. Depth is varied. The water is extremely shallow toward the east. Visibility ranges from 5 to 15 feet.

Dive Profile

The main attraction of this dive is the number of crab that inhabit the area. You can dive anywhere around the islands and find lots of Dungeness crab and rock crab. There are large sea lemon nudibranchs and pink tipped nudibranchs here. Little brooding anemones in reds and browns and greens cling to the blades of eel grass. You will likely see cabezon and dogfish. We enjoyed watching the bizarre looking ratfish and found a big skate about four feet across.

It is a good idea to use a compass because the bottom all looks the same and there are not any natural underwater landmarks for navigation. The current is never so strong that you cannot swim against it.

Directions

Hat Island is 0.86 of a mile (106 deqrees) from Southeast Point, Guemes Island, and 2.17 miles (81 degrees) from the Stack in Anacortes. Saddlebag is 0.39 of a mile (331 degrees) from Hat Island. You can launch your boat at Deception Pass, Flounder Bay, Washington Park, or Cap Sante in Anacortes.

The northern cove at Saddlebag Island has the best anchorage. There are campsites and fireplaces for cooking your crab.

Hat and Saddleback Islands were named for their physical configurations.

Hazards

Spring and fall tides are heavy. The big hazards here are boats, boats, boats. In the summer, you can almost walk from one to another. They come for the crab and the salmon fishing.

If you plan to continue across Rosario Strait, a stop at your favorite dive shop or any marina in the area will put you in touch with the latest wind and weather conditions.

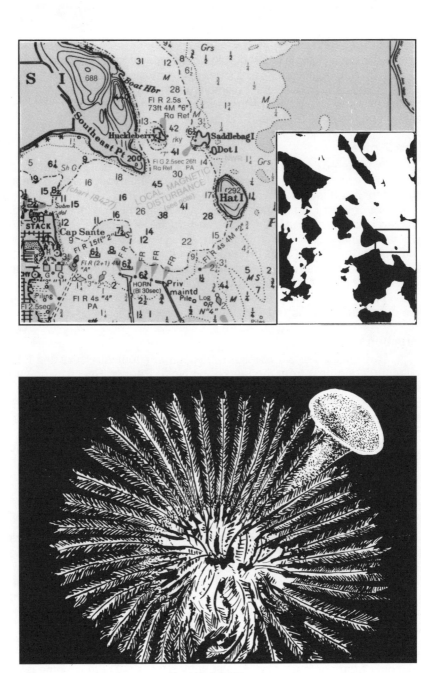

Red Tube Worm

Habitat and Depth

Lawrence Point is located at the eastern tip of Orcas Island. It is a rocky area with many cracks and small caves. Visibility ranges from 20 to 40 feet. You can choose your maximum depth. The water becomes more shallow as you move toward the northwest part of the island. Kelp is present on the point and along the bank.

Dive Profile

We entered the water just northwest of the point on the end of a falling tide. The majority of our dive was in 40 to 60 feet, although we did reach 80 feet for five minutes.

We dove around the point which is an excellent area for big lingcod. We saw a couple hidden in the caves and cracks. All kinds of rockfish also live here: canary, quillback, and copper, along with greenling, basket stars and Puget Sound king crab. The rocks shelter pecten and rock scallops, abalone, giant red sea urchins, and alabaster nudibranchs. Octopuses and wolfeels live in the cracks and crannies.

You will find fishing gear and a lot of lost cod jigs because of heavy use during the sport fishing season.

Directions

Lawrence Point is 5.13 Miles (290 degrees) from Viti Rocks and 1.13 miles (003 degrees) from the marker on North Peapod Rocks. You can launch your boat at Deception Pass, Flounder Bay, Washington Park, Cap Sante in Anacortes, or Bellingham. If you are ferrying your boat to the islands, you can launch at Rosario, Deer Harbor, Terrill Beach, or West Beach on Orcas Island.

The tidelands at Point Lawrence beach are public but there are no facilities there. Doe Island State Park is about 2.5 miles southwest. There are campsites, restrooms, a pier and moorage, and hiking trails. Water depth is shallow, so approach with caution.

Hazards

Do not be surprised at the thickness of the spring and fall fogs. Winds can make Rosario Strait and the Strait of Georgia quite rough in the afternoon. If you are on the West side of the Strait, it is just a short run through Peavine Pass or Thatcher Pass to the protected waters on the inside of Blakely and Decatur Islands. The east sides of Cypress and Guemes Islands will provide you with enough wind protection to allow for a safe run back to Anacortes.

Strong current is your major diving hazard here. Visibility reduces with a heavy current. Often the current will run in one direction and the wind will come from another. This results in high waves. There is some boat traffic.

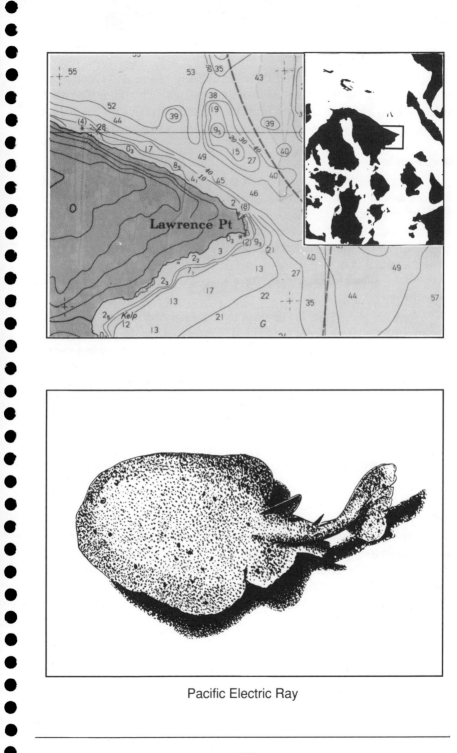

Pacific Electric Ray

Habitat and Depth

Peavine Pass is located between Blakely Island and Obstruction Island. The reef is on the east side of the pass and is marked. The north side is a rocky area with unlimited maximum depth. Visibility is 10 to 30 feet. The kelp bed which runs south of the rocks is good for shallow diving.

Dive Profile

We began the dive on the north side. Following the rocky wall down, we saw lots of anemones, white, green, tiny zoanthids, rock and pecten scallops, and red sea gherkins. There were some large basket stars. We also found an octopus out and about. Fish were plentiful: cabezon, kelp greenling, perch, rockfish, and lingcod. We swam around to the south and dove the kelp bed before coming up.

Directions

Peavine Pass Reef is identified by a marker on the reef. It is on the east side of the pass. Peavine Pass is located 3.43 miles (297 degrees) from Strawberry Island and 4.04 miles (249 degrees) from the marker on Cypress Reef. You can launch your boat at Deception Pass, Flounder Bay, Washington Park, Cap Sante in Anacortes, or Bellingham. If you are ferrying your boat to the islands, you can launch at Rosario, Deer Harbor, Terrill Beach, or West Beach, all on Orcas Island.

There are four public beaches on Blakely Island, but they have no improvements and the area above the tidelands is all privately owned. A better choice for a stop might be one of the many bays and coves around Orcas Island.

Hazards

Use caution when you run into heavy fog during the spring and fall. Winds can make Rosario Strait quite rough in the afternoon. If you are on the west side of the strait, head through Peavine Pass or Thatcher Pass to the protected waters on the inside of Blakely and Decatur Islands. The east sides of Cypress and Guemes Islands give enough wind protection to allow for a safe run back to Anacortes.

The current through the pass can run from 5.5 to 6.5 knots. Be alert for it. This is not a good area for a novice boater. You must be able to read the currents and water movement. Kelp has to be avoided. A sounder is a good idea because of the shallowness of Peavine Pass.

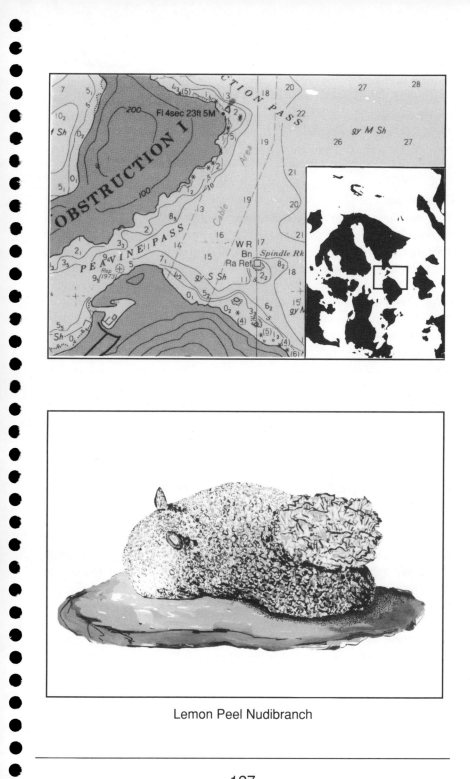

Lemon Peel Nudibranch

Habitat and Depth

This bone-shaped island is not to be confused with the Strawberry Island near Deception Pass. This one is 400 yards off Strawberry Bay on the west side of Cypress Island. There is a rock wall with wide ledges. You can choose your own maximum depth. Visibility ranges from 20 to 30 feet. There is some kelp.

Dive Profile

We entered the water at the northwest end of the island and drifted south with the slight current. The wall drops down about 60 to 70 feet from the surface and then forms ledges about 50 feet wide. It drops again to 130 feet and then gradually slopes down.

If you enjoy scallops, there are lots of both pectens and rock scallops here. There are many varieties of sea urchins, with green and purple the most abundant. You will find some Puget Sound king crab and basket stars. We saw quillback and copper rockfish and some lingcod. Below the second dropoff are many octopuses and wolfeels that feed on the pecten scallops. You'll also find a lot of lost fishing gear.

Directions

Strawberry Island is 1.3 miles (334 degrees) from Reef Point, Cypress Island, and 2.86 miles (151 degrees) from Lydia Shoal. You can launch your boat at Deception Pass, Flounder Bay, Washington Park, or Cap Sante in Anacortes. If you are driving to the islands, you can launch at Roche Harbor Boatel, Snug Harbor Marina, or San Juan County Park, all on San Juan Island; or Rosario, Deer Harbor, or Northwest Shore on Orcas Island; or Lummi Island.

Strawberry Island was originally named after a variety of strawberry, but in time it was the generic term that stuck. It has a sandy cove on the southeast neck of the "bone." However, only small boats or kayaks can land there.

Hazards

Heavy fog during the spring and fall is a consideration. Winds can make Rosario Strait quite rough in the afternoon. The east sides of Cypress and Guemes Islands will provide you with enough wind protection to allow for a safe run back to Anacortes. Be aware of the currents which can pose some problems. As you would expect, there can be a lot of boat traffic during the sport fishing season.

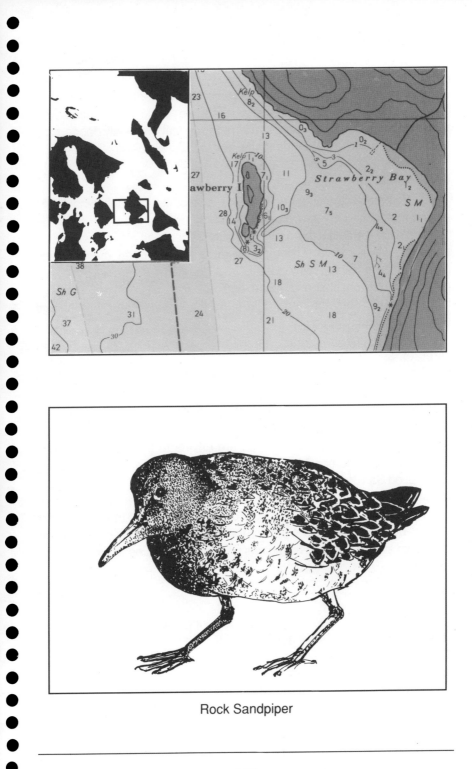

Rock Sandpiper

Habitat and Depth

Towhead Island is about 400 yards off the north end of Cypress Island. The south and west sides are shale. You can choose your maximum depth. Visibility ranges from 15 to 20 feet and really depends on the current. Try to dive on the high slack for best visibility.

Dive Profile

We entered the water on the north side of the island just inside the eleven fathom line as shown on NOAA chart 18421.

We have enjoyed this area on every dive because of the great variety of life you will see here. Living on the rocks are cup coral, giant red and purple urchins, white, pink-tipped, and zoanthid anemones, red sea gherkins, gum boot chiton, abalone, and rock scallops. Red rock crab and blood stars are common here. There are many varieties of rockfish and some nice sized lingcod.

Directions

Towhead Island is 0.17 of a mile (353 degrees) north of Cypress Island. It is 0.26 of a mile (105 degrees) from Cypress Reef and 1.73 miles (205 degrees) from the marker north of Boulder Reef. You can launch your boat at Deception Pass, Flounder Bay, Washington Park, Cap Sante in Anacortes, or in Bellingham. If you are driving to the islands, you can launch at Roche Harbor Boatel, Snug Harbor Marina, or San Juan County Park; all on San Juan Island, or at Rosario, Deer Harbor, Northwest Shore on Orcas Island, or Lummi Island.

The dock at the south end of Towhead Island and the uplands are private, but the tidelands are public. Pelican Beach Recreation Site on the northeast side of Cypress Island has camping, picnicking, restrooms, and moorage.

Hazards

You may find heavy fog during the spring and fall. Winds can make Rosario Strait quite rough in the afternoon. The east sides of Cypress and Guemes Islands will provide you with enough wind protection to allow for a safe run back to Anacortes.

Watch for boat traffic. Sometimes the ferries will cut between Towhead and Cypress Island.

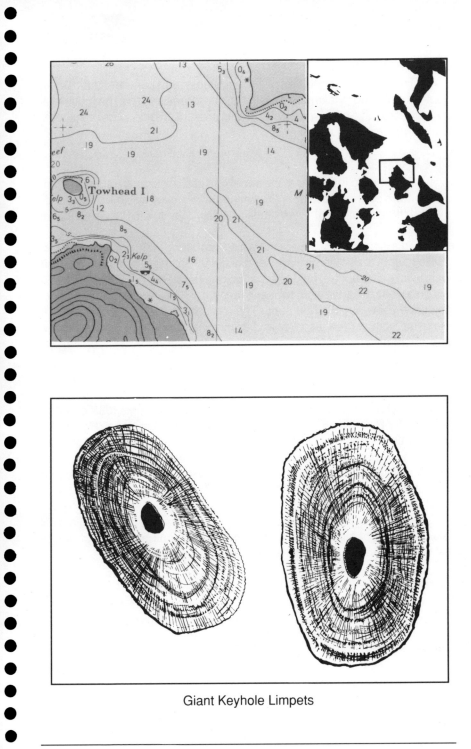

Giant Keyhole Limpets

Habitat and Depth

These rocks are located off the southeast tip of Lummi Island. Diving depth is unlimited. Maximum visibility is 20 - 30 feet, but it can be much less, so it is best to dive on a high slack. Kelp is present on both ends of the rocks as well as along the sides.

Dive Profile

We entered the water at the south end of the rocks on a slack ebb and swam north on the east side. The water temperature was much colder on this dive than on others that we made that day. We limited our depth to sixty feet.

This is an area of big boulders and good drop-offs. You will find rock scallops, lots of pecten scallops, and quillback, china, and brown rockfish. Octopuses and wolfeels hide in the rocks. There are big lingcod here. It is a good idea to carry a light to seek them out as they hide in the dark space and caves between the boulders. The rocks themselves are covered with the usual complement of white and green anemones, cup coral, bryozoa, and encrusting sponge. Striped and lemon peel nudibranchs also add color.

Directions

Viti Rocks is SSE of Lummi Island. It is 0.73 of a mile (233 degrees) from Carter Point and 5.13 miles (110 degrees) from Lawrence Point. You can launch your boat at Deception Pass, Flounder Bay, Washington Park, Cap Sante in Anacortes, or Bellingham. If you are driving to the islands, you can launch at Roche Harbor Boatel, Snug Harbor Marina, or San Juan County Park, all on San Juan Island; or at Rosario, Deer Harbor or Northwest Shore on Orcas Island.

Strange as it may seem, Viti Rocks are named after one of the Fiji Islands. Lummi Island Recreation Site on the southeast side of Lummi Island has nice beaches and a pretty setting for a lunch stop.

Hazards

There can be heavy fog in the spring and fall. Winds can make Rosario Strait and the Strait of Georgia quite rough in the afternoon. The east sides of Cypress and Guemes Islands will provide you with enough wind protection to allow for a safe run back to Anacortes.

Dive Viti Rocks on a nice day. It always seems to be windy here and the water gets quite choppy in any kind of breeze. The major hazards here are current and lots of fishing nets.

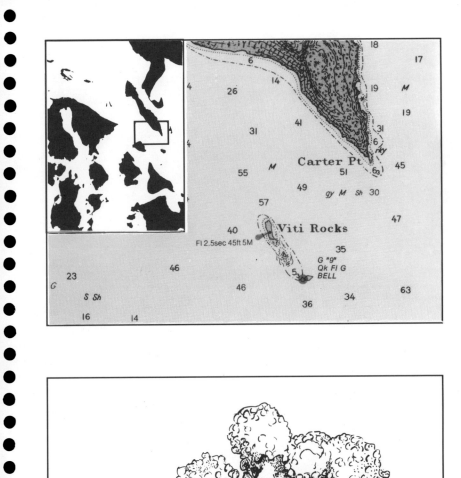

Red Soft Coral

INDEX BY DIVE SITE

Alden Point (Zone 4), 80-81
Allan Island (Zone 1), 10-11
Battleship Island (Zone 3), 54-55
Belle Rocks (Zone 2), 30-31
Bellevue Point (Zone 3), 56-57
Bird Rocks (Zone 2), 32-33
Burrows Island (Zone 1), 12-13
Boundary Pass Marker Buoy
    (Zone 4), 82-83
Carter Point (Zone 5), 112-113
Center Reef (Zone 3), 58-59
Charles Point (Zone 3), 60-61
Colville Island (Zone 2), 34-35
Cone Island (Zone 5), 114-115
Cypress Reef (Zone 5), 116-117
Davidson Rock (Zone 2), 36-37
Deception Island (Zone 1), 14-15
Deception Pass (Zone 1), 16-17
Dennis Shoals (Zone 1), 18-19
Eagle Cliff (Zone 5), 118-119
Eagle Point, Matia Island
    (Zone 4), 84-85
Eagle Point, San Juan Island
    (Zone 3), 62-63
Eliza Rock (Zone 5), 120-121
Ewing Island (Zone 4), 86-87
Fidalgo Head (Zone 1), 20-21
Flattop Island (Zone 4), 88-89
Goose Island (Zone 2), 38-39
Hat/Saddlebag (Zone5), 122-123
Ilceberg Point (Zone 2), 40-41
James Island (Zone 2), 42-43
Johns Island (Zone 3), 64-65
Johnson Island (Zone 4), 90-91
Jones Island (Zone 4), 92-93
Kellett Bluff (Zone 3), 66-67

Kellett Ledge (Zone 2), 44-45
Lawrence Point (Zone 5),
    124-125
Lawson Bluff (Zone 4), 94-95
Lawson Reef (Zone 1), 22-23
Lawson Rocks (Zone 2), 46-47
Lime Kiln (Zone 3), 68-69
Long Island (Zone 2), 48-49
Lopez Pass (Zone 2), 50-51
Low Island (Zone 3), 70-71
McCracken Point (Zone 3), 72-73
Parker Reef (Zone 4), 96-97
Peavine Pass (Zone 5), 126-127
Pile Point (Zone 3), 74-75
Point Disney (Zone 4), 98-99
Point Doughty (Zone 4), 100-101
Puffin Island (Zone 4), 102-103
Raccoon Point (Zone 4), 104-105
Sares Head (Zone 1), 24-25
Skipjack Island (Zone 4), 106-107
Spieden Bluff (Zone 3), 76-77
Strawberry Island (Zone 5),
    128-129
Toe Point (Zone 4), 108-109
Towhead Island (Zone 5),
    130-131
Turn Point (Zone 3), 78-79
Vita Rocks (Zone 5), 132-133
West Point (Zone 1), 26-27
Whale Rocks (Zone 2), 52-53
White Rock (Zone 4), 110-111
Williamson Rocks (Zone 1), 28-29

Are you interested in being on a mailing list to receive information on future publications in the Evergreen Pacific Dive Series?

COMING SOON

Puget Sound Shore Dives, revised edition

Diving the Shipwrecks in Washington Waters

AND MORE . . .

Cut out and return the postcard below and you will receive information on how you can purchase future Evergreen Dive books at a prepublication discount.

Please place my name on your mailing list to receive more information on furture publications in the **Evergreen Pacific Dive Series** and how I can obtain a prepublication discount on these publications.

Name _____

Address _____

City _____

State _____ Zip _____

Please
Place
Stamp
Here

Evergreen Pacific
Publishing
18002 15th Avenue N.E., Suite B
Seattle, WA 98155